MODERN DRAMATISTS

MODERN DRAMATISTS

MODERN AND POST-MODERN MIME

Thomas Leabhart

St. Martin's Press   New York

First published in the United States of America in 1989

Printed in Hong Kong

ISBN 0–312–02346–4

Library of Congress Cataloging-in-Publication Data

Leabhart, Thomas.
    Modern and post-modern mime / Thomas Leabhart.
        p.   cm.—(Modern dramatists)
    Bibliography: p.
    Includes index.
    ISBN 0–312–02346–4: $35.00 (est.)
    1. Mimes—Biography.   2. Mime—History—20th century.
3. Pantomime.   I. Title.   II. Series.
PN1986.A2L44 1989
792.3'028'0922—dc19
[B]
                                            88–19930
                                                CIP

Contents

List of Plates

Photograph © M. H. Dasté.

11. The Vieux Colombier company performing *Les Four- beries de Scapin* outdoors in the Place St Sulpice, Paris, c. 1920.
    Photograph © M. H. Dasté.

12. Director, teacher, actor and theatre visionary Jacques Copeau.
    Photograph © French Embassy Press and Information Division, N.Y.C.

13. Deburau as Pierrot by Maurice Sand.
    © Bibliothèque de l'Arsenal, Paris.

14. Pierrot with long sleeves by Maurice Sand.
    © Bibliothèque de l'Arsenal, Paris.

15. Ink drawing of Jean-Gaspard Deburau by Michael Tomek, based on lithographs in the Bibliothèque de l'Arsenal.
    © *Mime Journal.*

16. French mime Marcel Marceau teaching class.
    Photograph © Rebecca Knight.

17. French mime Marcel Marceau as Bip.
    Unattributed photograph.

18. Marcel Marceau in performance.
    Photograph © Gapihan.

19. Jacques Lecoq teaching with the help of leather masks by Amleto Sartori.
    Photograph © *The Glasgow Herald.*

20. Jacques Lecoq.
    Photograph © Patrick Lecoq.

21. A Mummenschanz full-body mask from their second show.
    Photograph © Christian Altorfer.

22. A moment from the first Mummenschanz show.
    Photograph © Gapihan.

For Sally

Editors' Preface

Modern Dramatists is an international series of introductions to major and significant nineteenth- and twentieth-century dramatists, movements and new forms of drama in Europe, Great Britain, America and new nations such as Nigeria and Trinidad. Besides new studies of great and influential dramatists of the past, the series includes volumes on contemporary authors, recent trends in the theatre and on many dramatists, such as writers of farce, who have created theatre 'classics' while being neglected by literary criticism. The volumes in the series devoted to individual dramatists include a biography, a survey of the plays, and detailed analysis of the most significant plays, along with discussion, where relevant, of the political, social, historical and theatrical context. The authors of the volumes, who are involved with theatre as playwrights, directors, actors, teachers and critics, are concerned with the plays as theatre and discuss such matters as performance, character interpretation and staging, along with themes and contexts.

BRUCE KING
ADELE KING

xi

Acknowledgements

The author is deeply grateful for the help he has had at every step in the writing of this book, especially from series editors Bruce and Adele King, and Graham Eyre. My colleague at Pomona College, Leonard Pronko, has read the manuscript and made valuable suggestions, as have specialists and friends elsewhere: Marlene Chatterton, Barbara Leigh, Annette Lust, Bari Rolfe and Laurence Senelick. Marie-Hélène Dasté has provided invaluable insight and information, encouraging me even when my conclusions have not matched her own. Birgit Olsen, Francis McLean and Arthur Feinsod have allowed me to use their unpublished interviews and research. Gina Lalli provided me with archival material from Decroux's New York school; Jim Calder gave me insights into Lecoq's teaching. Peter Bu's essay 'Mimes, Clowns and the 20th Century?' in *New Mime in Europe* and Theodore F. Wolff's art criticism in the *Christian Science Monitor* have afforded me new perspectives; Virginia Goodermont has helped me become computer literate. The Pomona College Faculty Research Committee has generously supported this undertaking. My wife, Sally Leabhart, has collaborated throughout, taking time away from her own work to share in mine.

Introduction:
Mime and Pantomime

The name Marcel Marceau has been synonymous with mime during recent decades, and, although he plays a small part in this book, it is thanks to his extensive touring since the early 1950s that much of the recent widespread interest in this ancient art is due. He and mimes such as the Mummenschanz company are the most visible elements of a return to expressive movement which has manifestations in the contemporary theatre of Grotowski, Mnouchkine, Peter Brook and others. These individuals and groups who command the attention of the theatre world derive from a tradition that is traceable to the early years of this century and the revolutionary work of French teacher and director Jacques Copeau, passing down from him to his pupil Etienne Decroux and to Decroux's students Jean-Louis Barrault and Marcel Marceau. Teachers Jean Dasté and Jacques Lecoq derive directly from Copeau's school as well. I shall have to distinguish between an earlier nineteenth-

1

century silent pantomime tradition, by which Marceau is strongly influenced, and modern mime, which uses sounds and words as well as movement metaphor. As the better-known pantomime tradition avoids sounds and words, it will be useful to outline briefly the history of mime until the early twentieth century and Copeau.

The issue of silence in mime is an important one. Must mime be silent? Brendan Gill wrote in the *New Yorker* of 28 March 1983.

> At the heart of pantomime is the sublimated anguish of lost speech; even as we are being entertained, we measure that loss and feel for the mute performer the sympathy aroused by any profound inescapable defect. To be in the presence of an imposed, unnatural silence is in effect to be rendered deaf; if Marceau didn't take care to have music accompany his exquisite unspoken narratives, I wonder whether we wouldn't soon find them unbearable.

It would seem, however, that most mime, from earliest times to the present, has been accompanied by sound of some kind: speech supplied by a narrator, chorus, or the mime performer; percussive sounds produced by striking one part of the body against another or the floor; or the kind of vocal mime Copeau's students experimented with, using pre- and post-verbal warbles and chortles and other expressive sounds that are not words. In 1890 a papyrus scroll was found that contained the scripts for thirteen mime plays written by Herondas, a Greek writer who lived in Alexandria around 270 BC (see *The Mimes of Herondas*, tr. Guy Davenport, 1981). These lively, colourful and sometimes ribald miniature dramas appear to confirm that in the ancient world at least some performers

2

called mimes spoke, and even memorised texts written by others. And, while pantomime performers (as distinct from mime performers) did not speak themselves, their performances were rarely unaccompanied by speech, song and instrumental music. Some antique poets also recited their own works, and accompanied the recitation with expressive gesture. Legend has it that one Livius Andronicus, upon losing his voice in 240 BC, hired an actor to recite for him while he continued the gestural part of his performance. If this story is apocryphal, someone felt a need to invent it to explain why individual mime performers might be silent, whether from adversity or aesthetic choice, while the performances themselves usually had some verbal as well as musical component.

A book published in Paris in 1751 entitled *Recherches historiques et critiques sur les mimes et sur les pantomimes* indicates by its title that the author, Jacques Méricot, thought there was some difference between the two terms 'mime' and 'pantomime', so frequently used interchangeably now. Méricot opined that pantomime was entirely silent while the mime performer was accompanied by an actor who spoke for him. This separation allowed the person who moved to exert himself more fully, and the person who spoke to speak without loss of breath. Such an arrangement leads one to speculate that perhaps the earliest Bharata Natyam (dance-drama of South India) performers were storytellers who illustrated their stories with gesture and dance, and that, as the dance became more complex and athletic, the vocal parts were taken up by professional singers.

M. Willson Disher attributes the current assumption that pantomime is silent to the Duchesse du Maine, who in 1706, wanting to add to the glories of the *Nuits de Sceaux*, decided to present the fourth act of Corneille's 'Horace' as a ballet by Mouret to be danced by Ballon [who had such a good jump that lightness in dancing has ever since been known as *ballon*] and Prévot. Out of literary conceit she called it a 'ballet-pantomime'. Her claim was that dumb-show was an art belonging to the ancients. No *savant* pointed out that 'imitator of all' does not signify speechlessness. . . . The gallant lexicographers of England have, from that day to this, insisted that pantomime means dumb-show for no other reason than the Duchess du Maine said it was so.   (1925, p. 225)

Although in most periods mime and pantomime have included some form of speech produced either by a primary or secondary performer, as well as music and percussive sounds produced by the performers or musicians, there were some important periods in which pantomime was without spoken text because of government sanctions forbidding it in certain theatres. These restrictions resulted in a form of performance which can be beautiful and complete in itself. But to expect, because of these relatively brief periods, that all mime should be silent is like assuming that all dancers should wear point shoes. Yet, as I write these words, most of the theatre-going public, most historians, and most mime performers will define mime as *silent* storytelling. Why?

Louis XIV expelled the Italian Players from Paris in 1697 because, it is said, they mocked his mistress, Madame de Maintenon. Rivalry between the Italian Players, on the one hand, and the Comédie Française and the Opéra (the King's theatres) on the other, grew to such a fervid pitch that the Italian Players (exiled to the Left Bank) were allowed by the authorities to play only on the condition that the actors not speak. By 1700 silent pantomime had been born, and the French had shown once more their genius for imposing arcane restrictions and then triumphantly devising ingenious ways of getting around them. In 1716 the ban was lifted, and the Italian Players were welcomed back to Paris; however, the number and *genre* of other theatres was still controlled. In 1750 the Boulevard du Temple, then on the fringes of Paris, became the official site of the fairground theatres, all of which were restricted in different ways: the first theatre licensed there was to present rope dancing only, and each subsequent one had another arduous limitation. The area soon took on a carnival atmosphere: animal acts, marionettes, jugglers, acrobats and harlequinades filled the streets, which were lined with cabarets and cafés. It must have looked much like the portrait of it painted in the film *Les Enfants du paradis*. Perhaps the most absurd restriction was the one that required actors to perform behind a gauze screen; when the actor Plancher-Valcour heard, on 14 July 1789, that the Bastille had been stormed, he broke through the gauze curtain shouting, 'Long live liberty!' (Root-Bernstein, 1984, p. 178).

In England in 1717, the actor John Rich was attracted to this French novelty as he was less able in speech than in gesture. He soon popularised the new silent pantomime in England, and English innovations in turn influenced the French. Soon itinerant pantomime troupes were performing thoughout France, Holland, Germany, Austria and Denmark.

Legal restrictions determining repertoire, cast size, number of musicians, and whether dialogue or song could be added to pantomime continued in France until 1791, but popular entertainment flourished despite official sanctions, and thirty-five theatres had sprung up on the Boulevard du Temple by that date. The number subsequently grew to one hundred after the National Assembly ratified decrees in January 1791 permitting any citizen to establish a public theatre and to present plays of any kind. At that time, dialogue and song, which had been the privilege of the King's theatres alone, were immediately added to pantomimes to produce a new hybrid called 'melodrama' (Carlson, 1974, p. 27).

Restrictions were reimposed in 1807 by Napoleon, who regulated the number of theatres in Paris as well as their *genre* and repertoire, and Jean-Gaspard Deburau began his meteoric career in 1819 at the Théâtre des Funambules on the Boulevard du Temple. The dynasty he established continued through the early 1920s, even though restrictions on speech were lifted in Deburau's lifetime.

By the end of the nineteenth century in France, academic rigidity had crept into theatre, mime and dance. The genius of Deburau had been replaced by a long succession of imitators who re-created the outward form, but had lost the inner fire; pantomime was an affair of the hands and face, the body covered by voluminous garments. The dance at the Paris Opéra, reduced to musical statue-posing, relied heavily on the extremities of the body, as the torso was rigidly corseted. Theatre at that time was an exaltation of the personalities of certain star performers, who surrounded themselves with mediocre supporting actors. The time was ripe for change, and, if things were not quite as bad as the revolutionaries made them out to be, there was at least some truth in claims that renewal was imperative. This renewal, however, came not from within the arts in question, but as a result of the new interests in science, technology and sport. The nineteenth century's preoccupation with 'establishing and describing . . . the true facts of animal locomotion in general and

6

human locomotion in particular' (Sparshott, Foreword
to Souriau, 1983, p. ix) can be seen in the work of independent movement researchers, whose work, begun in
the nineteenth century, was to have a telling effect on
twentieth-century mime, theatre and dance.

Eadweard Muybridge, born Edward Muggeridge in
1830 in England, began photographing movement in Palo
Alto, California, in 1872, when Leland Stanford, a former
California governor, provided funds for Muybridge to
photograph Stanford's racehorse to see if all four feet ever
left the ground simultaneously. In these experiments,
Muybridge developed a technique of using twenty-four
cameras to take sequential action photos. He continued
this research at the University of Pennsylvania, where he
was sponsored by the painter Thomas Eakins, and by 1885
he had produced 100,000 photographs of horses, domestic
and wild animals, and human beings. His work, and that
of the Frenchman Jules Marey, author of *La Machine
animale*, used new technologies to expand knowledge of
movement into areas beyond normal human perception.
Muybridge lectured in the United States and in Europe
using a zoopraxiscope, a device he invented to show glass
slides in quick succession, creating the effect of movement.
In 1887 he published *Animal Locomotion*, in 1899 *Animals
in Motion*, and in 1901 *The Human Figure in Motion*. His
documentation of what happened in natural movement
was a revelation to those whose profession was the
depiction of this movement in stylised and theatrical ways.
Thomas Eakins was dismissed from his job as teacher at
an art school for using nude models; within the next
quarter of a century, almost nude dancers and mimes
would perform on the stage. Sculptors such as Rodin in
France chose to work with nude models in motion rather
than from the plaster casts from which one learned to

7

draw in the academies. Isadora Duncan performed for Rodin, who drew while she danced in his studio.

The French philosopher Paul Souriau, was born in 1852. Like Muybridge, he attempted to understand movement, but with philosophy instead of the camera as his tool. One of his principal works was entitled *The Aesthetics of Movement*. Souriau understood his contemporary Gustave Eiffel, who had asked,

> Do not actual conditions of strength always conform to the secret conditions of harmony? The first principle of architectural aesthetics is that the essential lines of a movement be determined by their perfect appropriateness to their intent.
>
> (Quoted in 1983, Souriau, p. 100)

This voices the spirit that destroyed the nineteenth century's academies.

François Delsarte taught voice, public speaking and stage acting in Paris from 1839 until 1871. At the age of fourteen he was admitted to the Conservatoire in Paris to study voice, despite his youth and the demanding entrance requirements of that institution. Within six months, as a result of improper teaching, he had lost his voice. Undaunted, he set out to discover a science behind the art. He criticised the Conservatoire training of the day as mere parroting of the professor, and observed that the professors were often in disagreement. He found that 'no theory supported the execution' and he set out on the 'conquest of the science which was to make me a great artist' (Stebbins, 1977, pp. 44–5). Delsarte's teachings would have to travel to the United States and, through Ted Shawn, Ruth St Denis, and Isadora Duncan, influence American modern dance before they would finally have some effect on the dancing at the Paris Opéra a quarter of a century later. Shawn, St Denis and Isadora performed almost nude at times, and their daring experiments in loose-fitting, free-flowing garments were in direct opposition to the clothing-styles and the morality of their time. Their example helped free the bodies of men and women from corsets, shoes and other binding clothing, and, something we do not often remember, reminded people how gracefully and beautifully the body could move when it was not restrained. They embodied Muybridge's images, connecting his still photographs of nude men and women with movement more fluid than his zoopraziscope had been able to produce. The application of Delsarte's principles liberated the torso as an expressive element, permitting undulation through that previously rigidly held part of the body. The tension–relaxation dynamic scale of modern dance, based on Delsarte's law of reaction–recoil is comparable to the principle of muscular respiration found in modern mime. The creative use of mass, weight and gravity is as important in modern mime as it is in modern dance. Shawn's contention that the abstract movements of modern dance are based on concrete gestures echoes Decroux's statement that 'The abstract is the flower of the concrete.' Even Decroux's lifelong concern with counterweights has a corollary in Delsarte's law of equilibrium, which outlines four types of adjustments the body makes in response to certain exertions (Shawn, 1954, pp. 64, 71).

A cult of gymnastics swept Europe in the nineteenth century (to keep the population in good shape for war and as an antidote to physically debilitating work in factories), and, when Copeau set up his school in the early 1900s, one of the leading French exponents of this still important movement was Lieutenant Georges Hébert.

Hébert developed a system of physical education and movement analysis which Copeau included in the curriculum of the Ecole du Vieux Colombier in 1922–3 (Leigh, 1979, p. 34). Hébert's *L'Education physique de l'entraînement complète par la méthode naturelle* includes stage-by-stage diagrams (*à la* Muybridge) of the natural way to perform sports movements. Some years later Etienne Decroux created a substantial number of teaching models for his modern-mime technique through analysis of sports movements in this frame-by-frame way.

Paul Bellugue, who was professor of anatomy at the Ecole des Beaux Arts in Paris from 1936 until 1955, is the last of our major figures who helped pave the way for modern mime. Bellugue often gave lecture demonstrations on dance and sports with the assistance of Etienne Decroux, who illustrated certain of the principles Bellugue described. When Bellugue writes, 'Beauty is the visible form of economical gesture', he echoes Souriau quoting Eiffel. Both Decroux and Jacques Lecoq, who began his career as a teacher of physical education and physical therapy, quote Bellugue often and easily. Bellugue spent a good part of his career in the analysis of sports as well as of dance and sculpture. His statement that 'The culture of the dancer and of the athlete rest on the same principles, simplifying, purifying, and ordering gestures' (Bellugue, n.d., p. 110) is one with which both Decroux and Lecoq would readily agree.

The industrial revolution of the nineteenth century naturally created interest in the analysis of movement as a way of establishing efficient interaction between man and the machine. It is not surprising that artists were in turn led to create expressive movement based on this research, as in Decroux's *L'Usine* and in countless other

10

futurist, constructivist and Bauhaus *ballets méchaniques*. Jean-Louis Barrault has written,

> Let us not hesitate to say it: there should be, deep in every actor, an element of the robot. The function of art is to lead this robot toward the natural; to proceed by artificial means toward an imitation of nature. It is because the violin is a hollow box, like a dead body, that it is so satisfying to furnish it with a soul.
>
> (Barrault, 1949, p. 29)

This sounds very much like Paul Souriau describing the three qualities required of movement in order to have aesthetic value: 'mechanical beauty of movement, its expression, and the perceptible pleasure it gives' (1983, p. xx).

Most important of all to an understanding of contemporary theatre and contemporary mime is the work of Jacques Copeau. Copeau reacted strongly against what he saw to be the decadence of the theatre in Paris in the early 1900s. In order to overcome the weakness he knew to be inherent in the star system, with its ham acting and insensitive treatment of texts, he proposed a new theatre with the 'renormalised' actor at its centre. This 'renormalised' actor had to be trained to unlearn all the artificiality he had consciously and unconsciously acquired. In order to produce the sort of actors he required, Copeau founded the Ecole du Vieux Colombier, which had a curriculum calculated to give actors a much broader training than the narrowly specialised one meted out by the Conservatoire. Copeau's students studied literature, history, speech, voice and theatre crafts, and there was also a strong emphasis on physical training. Copeau believed that physical agility, mask work, ensemble acting and ability in mime were at the heart of the theatre's golden ages, the periods that had produced the Nō plays, Greek drama, the medieval mystery plays, the *commedia dell'arte*, and the plays of Molière and of Shakespeare. Physical training at the Ecole du Vieux Colombier involved acrobatics, classical ballet, gymnastics, sports and mask work, then known as corporeal mime.

The study of corporeal mime with Copeau at the Ecole du Vieux Colombier inspired Etienne Decroux to devote his life to research into the expressive possibilities of the human body after it had been freed from the tyranny of what Decroux called the 'alien arts' of literature, scenery, music, dance, costuming and so on. Decroux, however, never intended the theatre to remain without a voice; he proscribed ordinary speech for a thirty-year period, or until the actor had taken command of his own house, at which time the alien arts could be reintroduced as required, the actor firmly in control.

Decroux, reacting strongly against the white-faced pantomime he had seen at *café-concerts* as a child, envisioned a modern mime which would be as clear and beautiful a record of essence as are the paintings of Mondrian and the sculpture of Brancusi, two of Decroux's contemporaries. And, although Decroux initially worked with pantomime illusions (objective mime), his later work was to be more subjective, exploring ways of expressing the movement of thought, studying the way thought shaped the body, and examining in great detail the way physical exertion shaped the body (counterweights). The Promethean struggle of man against gravity as it is individualised in any specific dramatic situation has been central to Decroux's work, which has been, for fifty years, diametrically opposed to charming or humorous entertainments. Although Decroux had a long and successful career as a stage, screen and radio actor, his mime performances did not meet with wide public acclaim, perhaps because of their tendency toward the abstract, non-linear structure one finds in most modernist work in other arts. Decroux's greatest contribution to mime has been as a master teacher, inventor of the corporeal-mime technique, and theoretician.

Jean-Louis Barrault worked closely with Decroux as he developed corporeal mime. Improvisation, to which Barrault brought great physical ability and considerable imagination, was a vital part of their work, and their early discoveries were catalogued and classified by Decroux. After a period of creative work using the discoveries of modern mime, including vocal mime, Barrault chose to continue his work in the speaking theatre.

Following the Second World War, another brilliant student of Decroux's began his career in mime. He was Marcel Marceau, who, after his studies with Decroux, developed a character named Bip who has more in common with the nineteenth-century paradigm of a white-faced silent pantomime than with the modern mime developed by Decroux. Marceau has become the most brilliant and well-known silent pantomime performer of our own or perhaps any time.

Just after the Second World War, Jacques Lecoq began as a teacher of physical education, and, through study with Jean Dasté and others who understood the theory and practice of the Ecole du Vieux Colombier, developed aspects of Copeau's rediscoveries in his own influential teaching. Lecoq has valued neutral and expressive mask work, improvisation and *commedia dell'arte*, and is primarily responsible for the rebirth of the clown as a theatre artist. His most recent research has focused on the *buffon*.

Silent performance is, of course, also associated with the early cinema, where the sweet adversity of limited technology provided a powerful stimulus to the careers of Chaplin, Keaton and a host of others. Ironically enough, it was a speaking film made during the German occupation of France in the mid-1940s which was to determine Marceau's career, and our current misconception of mime as 'silent storytelling'. *Les Enfants du paradis*, a classic created by Marcel Carné and Jacques Prévert, re-created the life and times of Jean-Gaspard Deburau. Starring in the film as Deburau was Jean-Louis Barrault, the French actor and mime who had studied with Decroux; Decroux also performed in the film as Deburau's father. In this tremendously popular and highly acclaimed film, Decroux and Barrault re-created the silent, white-faced illusionistic mime of an earlier period; we shall see how much at variance this depiction was with most of the modern-mime research Decroux and Barrault were then doing.

The young Marceau, a student of Decroux's in the late 1940s, when the film gained its first popular success, saw in it a vision of what his own career might become. True to his instinct, Marceau was to be for the twentieth century what Deburau had been for the nineteenth. Marceau drew heavily on the nineteenth-century French tradition as well as on the illusionistic mime research that Decroux was then doing but soon thereafter repudiated. The other primary source of Marceau's brilliant synthesis was the silent acting of Chaplin and Keaton.

Marceau's paradigm was to dominate the field, his name for decades synonymous with mime. Through various twists and turns of history, the brief periods in which mime was silent are recalled in his silent performance. The post-Marceau era in mime will most certainly see a return to the mainstream of this art. The mime one sees in international festivals the world over, the mime which derives primarily from the research and teaching of Lecoq and Decroux, is as far removed from 'silent storytelling' as can be imagined, and, as we have seen, in this it agrees with mime as it has been performed in most periods of history. Records from the Greek and Roman periods most often link mime and pantomime with spoken and sung narration, either by the mime performer or by another actor or a chorus. Certainly oriental theatres found early on that, as the vocal and the movement elements of performance became amplified and moved toward virtuosity, so it became increasingly necessary for them to be distributed among a number of performers each one of whom was a specialist rather than for a solo storyteller to do everything. Alternatively, where there was only one performer, the performance was best arranged so that, for example, the most demanding vocal part did not coincide with the most acrobatic movement.

During medieval times mime was often performed by strolling minstrels or wandering players, or as part of religious or secular drama. Again, it seems seldom to have been silent. The *commedia dell'arte*, a theatre form based on improvisation and containing lively and acrobatic movement as well as set and improvised dialogue, was immensely popular throughout Europe from the sixteenth to the eighteenth century. This theatre had much in common with the earlier types mentioned above: it was performed outdoors, used masks, and was the work of a usually itinerant ensemble working together in a closely knit family or family-like group.

Silent white-faced mime as we have come to know it made its first appearance in the 1820s, when Jean-Gaspard Deburau became the most popular performer of his time with his Baptiste pantomimes. He flourished in a theatre hemmed in by governmental restrictions imposed first by Louis XIV, continued throughout the reigns of Louis XV and Louis XVI, and later revived by Napoleon. These restrictions created silent pantomimes in which the necessary bits of text were supplied by cards or by songs sung by the audience, who followed the bouncing red ball along sheets of lyrics suspended above the silent performers. When these governmental restrictions were finally lifted before Deburau's death, the form in which he had excelled continued for some years, but by the early 1900s it had run its course, and the mainstream of theatrical activity consisted of melodramas, operettas and other popular entertainments using speech and song. The exaggerated movement style we so often associate with melodrama doubtless came about as a result of the period in which popular entertainments were deprived of speech.

Marceau and Deburau before him appear to have carried white-face illusionistic pantomime to its fullest extension; contemporary mime has returned to the model of synthesis as post-modern performers include speech, song and other theatrical elements in their work. In so doing, they begin to resemble the mimes of ancient and medieval times who spoke or who were accompanied by spoken or sung text, recited by choruses or narrators. As we examine mime from 1900 to the present, we discover that mime is not some precious and separate discipline quite outside the mainstream of theatre, but, rather, that it is again, as it used to be, a multi-faceted form of expression which is at the heart of theatre – a theatre of the creative actor who determines the synthesis of movement, text, music, lighting and decor. Mime is revealed as the cradle of movement, as well as of the vocal impulses through which the actor–creator first expresses internal states. Rather than a pleasant-enough diversion, a dumb-show, it is in fact the womb of theatre.

1
Jacques Copeau

Are we the representatives of a lost past? Are we, on the contrary, the precursors of a future which can hardly be discerned at the extreme limit of an ending era?

(Jacques Copeau)

In his much-cited book *The Structure of Scientific Revolutions*, Thomas Kuhn examines the nature of revolutions in scientific paradigms and the people who make them. Kuhn says that people thoroughly schooled in old paradigms are unable to distance themselves enough from them to see their flaws and inconsistencies. Hence it is often the amateur, the non-specialist or the outsider who has the objectivity needed to incorporate new information into a new world-view. Jacques Copeau was one of these outsiders and he knew it. He knew that when renewal had come to the theatre in the past it had often been thanks to the work of one who, at least at the beginning of his career, did not work in the mainstream theatre of the day.

17

Copeau cited examples to support this belief: Molière, Goethe, Antoine and Stanislavsky had each been, at one time, an amateur (in the French meaning, one who is a lover of an art rather than one who earns his living from that art) with a vision.

Copeau was born in 1879, attended the Lycée Condorcet, and later the Sorbonne. As a child he was taken by his grandfather to see the melodramas on the Boulevard du Temple, and later he attended Antoine's theatre. During a two-year sojourn in Denmark he produced his first literary and dramatic criticism, which was published in French literary magazines between 1901 and 1903. His father's death brought him back to France, where he tried without success to manage the family ironworks. He relocated happily in Paris, where he worked as a sales clerk in a modern art galley, becoming familiar with some of the most important painters and sculptors of his day. Although the pay was low, he was able to work in an artistic environment and to continue his writing. After a period of freelance work, he became the drama critic of the *Grande revue*. His growing revolutionary fervour for a new theatre was fuelled on one hand by the mediocrity of much of the theatre he saw day after day, and on the other hand by the men of letters he came to know at that time – extraordinary individuals who shared and helped to shape Copeau's convictions: André Gide, André Suarès and Charles Péguy. Copeau and his comrades wanted nothing less of theatre than a supreme art able to educate the public out of moral and intellectual decadence.

With Gide, Henri Ghéon, Jean Schlumberger, André Ruyters and Michel Arnaud, Copeau founded the *Nouvelle Revue Française* in 1909. The *NRF* symbolises the qualities Copeau valued above all else: classicism of form and of thought. His taste for purity, sobriety and harmonious

18

compromises between discipline and freedom was first expressed in the *NRF* and later demonstrated in the school and the theatre of the Vieux Colombier, whose early productions were called by a wit, who doubtless thought that Copeau had erred in the direction of discipline, the 'Folies Calvin'.

Copeau founded his Théâtre du Vieux Colombier in 1913, and its distinguishing feature was that it was formed by non-theatrical hands and minds. Copeau himself had worked as a writer, editor and critic until the age of thirty-three, at which time, never having set foot on stage, although he had written for and about it, he entered the theatre to test certain ideas he felt had been preparing themselves within his consciousness since childhood. Copeau wanted to save the theatre, and he was convinced that only those who were outside it could ensure its rejuvenation. He wanted to exercise his art without compromises based on lack of time, imagination, training, sincerity or integrity, compromises he found too frequent in the theatre of his day. Copeau repudiated the theatre as he knew it in favour of a vision that he and his associates had of theatre as they hoped it could be. To this ideal he considered that he had sacrificed everything – his literary career, his peace of mind, his material well-being, and his happy home. But he would never sacrifice his artistic vision. He wrote that, if ever there were a conflict between his theatre and his vision of it, it would be the theatre that would have to change and not his vision.

When Copeau read theatre history, he was dismayed to compare the theatre of his day with the grand periods that had gone before, to see how the great art of the Greeks and of Shakespeare had degenerated into popular amusement. The actors in the debased theatre of the early decades of the 1900s in Paris (except for the melodrama actors who played on the fringes of Paris) expressed themselves almost entirely through the voice and by facial expressions while the body remained relatively inexpressive. There were notable exceptions, of course: Sarah Bernhardt, although called the Voice of Gold, performed exceptionally agile and appropriate stage movement as well; but, as a star rather than a member of a dedicated and selfless ensemble, she represented another aspect of the decadence Copeau so detested.

To replace contemporary decadence, Copeau had an almost mystic vision of what theatre might become, and what it indeed had been in earlier times, in its noblest forms. Copeau wanted to restore to theatre the qualities he believed had been essential during theatre's golden ages. To achieve this goal, Copeau advocated renovation rather than revolution. It was a return to the former glories of Greece, the *commedia dell'arte*, the Elizabethans, that he recommended, not a forward movement into unknown territory. He believed that from time to time it was necessary to return to the very womb of theatre, to seek renewal of inner strength through the spirit that had animated the theatre at certain fecund periods in the past and could again animate it in the future.

The first part of this renewal for Copeau was a return to an empty, open performing space. Copeau worked out an equation that could be summarised in the words of another visionary in another field of endeavour: less is more. The reduction of theatre to its simplest, most basic and profound elements would purify it, strengthen it and enable it to reach the largest numbers of people and affect them on the deepest levels. This love of purity and simplicity is one of the most important hallmarks of the modernist movement and is to be found in the literature, music, poetry, painting and sculpture of Copeau's time.

This simplicity, while being modern, was ancient as well. The theatre structure Copeau saw as being the least complicated, and the most modern at the same time, was the Greek stage; the large number of theatres built without proscenium arches since Copeau's day amply substantiate his claim.

The simple circle of the Greek theatre, so ancient and so modern at the same time, immediately calls to mind the round threshing-floor of ancient times. And, while it is no longer gospel among classicists that the first theatres were in fact threshing-floors where workers danced when the harvest was over, it was just this unencumbered quality that attracted Copeau to both the Greek stage and the circus ring; in these similarly open spaces the imagination is able to wander freely, and decor is not an issue. In these spaces everything became the responsibility of the actor. Arthur Waley's *The Nō Plays of Japan* was an important book for Jacques Copeau. The oldest Nō stage therein depicted dates from 1464 and looks more like the old Globe or a Greek theatre than it does a proscenium playhouse (Waley, 1922, p. 13). The newer Nō stage depicted by Waley had the audience on two sides and a spareness of decor that allowed a great focus on the actor and his art (p. 15). Information such as this can only have confirmed Copeau's own convictions. Copeau's most quoted words are 'qu'on nous laisse un tréteau nu!' ('Give us a bare stage!'). He created the first presentational playhouse in the modern world by looking backward.

Copeau's strongly held convictions led him in 1913 to open the Théâtre du Vieux Colombier in Paris. Copeau chose the rue du Vieux Colombier to be as far away as possible from the conventional Parisian theatre (centred on the Comédie Française and *les grands boulevards*). He did not try to dissimulate his feelings of hatred for most plays, authors, directors, critics, actors, spectators and even ushers as found in those theatres. The revisions Copeau made in 1913 to the Théâtre du Vieux Colombier eliminated the proscenium and the footlights; in 1919, in collaboration with Louis Jouvet, he devised some of the first lighting-instruments which projected light from above the actor. Copeau's actor could, for the first time since theatre moved indoors, comport himself in relation to the light source (in this case artificial) in much the same way as earlier outdoor actors had, in relation to their (natural) light source. By taking away the proscenium arch, eliminating the footlights, adding a forestage over the orchestra pit and building steps into the audience, Copeau and Jouvet changed the rules for actors as well as for the audience for years to come.

Clearing the stage was the first and easiest task; peopling it with actors of presence, actors who did not disappear on such a stage, actors large enough to fill the empty space – that was the task Copeau would tackle with missionary zeal for the rest of his life. Copeau's theatre produced several important and popular productions in the 1913–14 season until interrupted by the First World War, when most of the actors, including two of the strongest members of the company, Dullin and Jouvet, were drafted. Copeau took advantage of the hiatus in theatre activities imposed by the war to visit theatre visionaries Gordon Craig, Jaques Dalcroze and Adolph Appia in 1915. The importance of these visits, coming as they did after Copeau had gained his first practical experiences of theatre-making, cannot be underestimated; while these men did not agree in every respect, they were at one in their desire for a complete renewal of theatre. Copeau certainly owed some of his vivid interest in the *commedia* and masks to Craig, some of his love of the bare stage and lighting to Appia, and some of his belief in the importance of physical training for the actor to Dalcroze.

In its first season the Vieux Colombier attracted a number of notable figures, including Rodin, Verhaeren, Bergson, Debussy and Clemenceau. It was owing to Clemenceau's support and interest that Copeau was asked by the French government to undertake a lecture tour of America as a French cultural ambassador, in order to influence American public opinion in favour of the French war effort. Thanks to the assistance of American millionaire Otto Kahn, the following year Copeau reassembled what he could of his company in New York, where, for two difficult years (1917–19), the young troupe produced more than fifty plays at the Garrick Theatre (twenty-five different plays in twenty-five weeks during the second year). Copeau was not happy with the quality of their work, as he felt that commercial pressures had limited their artistry; perhaps the troupe won a propaganda victory, however, by successfully counterbalancing a flourishing permanent German-language theatre in New York.

After the war, Copeau and company resumed productions at the rue du Vieux Colombier from 1919 to 1924. But the idea of a school was never far from Copeau's mind, as he began to realise more and more forcibly that the kind of actors he needed for his new theatre could only come from a school which was in itself as new and different as he hoped his theatre would be. In 1915 he had begun with Suzanne Bing, a leading actress in his company, the first attempts at a school, which were refined as Copeau redefined his objectives. His interests became more experimental and less production-oriented, until in 1924 the theatre closed while the school continued. The school was of more importance to the development of modern mime than was the theatre, yet the theatre reflected many of Copeau's highest ideals. Just as Duse's acting-style influenced Stanislavsky in his formulation of his method, so the acting-styles of Suzanne Bing, Louis Jouvet and Charles Dullin influenced Copeau's approach to teaching.

Dullin had his first success as an actor in *Les Frères Karamazov*, adapted and directed by Copeau. He would go on after his association with Copeau to nurture in his turn young promising actors at his own theatre, the Atelier. Louis Jouvet was also 'discovered' by Copeau. Jouvet, although he left the Vieux Colombier in 1922, inherited Copeau's actors and repertoire in 1924 when Copeau left Paris for Burgundy. Jouvet was a co-conspirator with Copeau in scenic as well as acting innovations. Both Dullin and Jouvet left their mark on Copeau's work and, later, on the corporeal-mime work of Etienne Decroux. Reviews of their work and of Copeau's own acting suggest that the qualities these actors had in common were a gift for dynamic immobility; a clear and coherent way of moving; a taste for sharp turns of the head or other isolated movements or gestures which drew focus; and a certain presence or charisma.

In Copeau's productions

gesture was . . . used sparingly and selectively, so that each gesture was given unusual significance. In Copeau's productions of classic comedies the acting had the balletic quality which so many producers attempt to achieve though the result is generally no more than a series of self-conscious posturings and caperings. At the Vieux Colombier the actors, as a result of their training,

seem to adopt this style naturally and spontaneously.
(Rudlin, 1986, p. 63)

These qualities were the ones Copeau valued, the ones he tried to teach his students, and are among those qualities which appear prominently in modern mime. But perhaps more important than any of these acting-qualities were the human ones that enabled actors to work together in an ensemble, to serve an art to which they had consecrated themselves.

Copeau railed against what in French is known as *cabotinage*. There is no exact English equivalent, although we might call it ham acting. It is perhaps a combination of, in equal parts, vulgarity, vanity, amorality and insincerity. For Copeau and his associates, art and morality were closely allied, and good art could not be produced by self-centred and egotistic people. To rid the actor of professional rigidity (to 'renormalise' him, in Copeau's terminology) and to give him a taste for working in an ensemble, Copeau's training stressed the importance of improvisation. Although now taken for granted in actor-training, like so many of Copeau's innovations, improvisation was an unheard-of technique of which there was no living tradition in the French theatre of the early 1900s. Another goal of improvisation was to release the actors' creative impulses so that they might escape from the dictatorial control of directors and playwrights and discover the suppleness of mind and body that their forebears, the actors of the *commedia dell'arte*, had possessed in such great measure. Copeau wanted actors to contribute collaboratively and equally with playwright and director; it is, after all, the actor who *acts*, who directly explores the role, while the playwright and director are usually sedentary. For Copeau, gymnastics, mime and dance had a vital role to play in increasing the actor's corporeal flexibility and so improving the ability to act. Not that Copeau ignored speech, but he felt that 'the spoken word, the articulated verb, [must] be the culmination of a thought felt by the actor in all his being, and the blossoming of both his interior state and of the bodily expression which translates it' (1974, pp. 114–15).

Copeau's Ecole du Vieux Colombier offered an extraordinary theatre education compared with what passed for actor-training at the Conservatoire at that time. Copeau was the father of the liberally educated whole actor, as opposed to the narrowly and professionally trained specialist typical of the mainstream theatre he so completely rejected. Copeau's conception of an actor's liberal education included, in addition to the courses listed above, classes in classical ballet, voice production, ordinary diction, declamation of classical chorus and of Japanese Nō, singing and sculpting; the history of music, costume, philosophy, literature, poetry and theatre; and corporeal mime.

Of all these classes, the only one which requires explanation is corporeal mime. The students called the class 'the mask', since for it they wore expressionless masks (at first, only a scarf wrapped over the face), the body as bare as decency would allow. Diminishing the potential of the face to communicate meant that the rest of the body would need to take on that role in addition to its own. This simple premise gave birth to modern mime.

In this almost nude, masked condition, the students improvised simple actions – a man trying to shoo away a fly; a woman strangling a fortune-teller; actions used in trade; a sequence of movements made by a machine. Sometimes these improvisations were preceded by a brief secret meeting among the participants to decide certain aspects of the work; at other times, however, Copeau would give a word – for example, 'Paris' – and the students would attempt, without reflection, to express what was suggested to them by that word. Copeau wanted his students to become astute observers of nature and of animals, performing exercises based on the birth of spring, the growth of plants, wind in the trees, the sunrise.

The manner of playing resembled the slow motion of film. But while that is the slowing down of fragments of reality, ours was the slow production of one gesture in which many others were synthesized.

(Decroux, 1985, p. 4)

It is significant that these exercises included sound as well as movement: 'We reproduced noises of the town, of the house, of nature, the cries of animals. All of this with the mouth, the hands and the feet' (ibid.).

In June 1924 the students of the Ecole du Vieux Colombier gave an end-of-term performance for an invited audience. Decroux, as he had only been at the school for a year, was not allowed to participate, but the performance marked him deeply. We might say that modern mime was conceived then and there.

Sitting quietly among the spectators, I beheld an astonishing show.

It consisted of mime and sounds. The whole performance took place without a word, without any make-up, without costumes, without a single lighting effect, without properties, without furniture and without scenery.

The development of the action was skillful enough for them to condense several hours into a few seconds, and to contain several places in only one. Simultaneously before our eyes we had the battlefield and civilian life, the sea and the city.

The characters moved from one to the other with total credibility.

The acting was moving and comprehensible, of both plastic and musical beauty.   (Ibid., pp. 4–5)

When Decroux wrote of 'plastic and musical beauty' he was referring to beautiful bodily attitudes, and the varied dynamic qualities with which they changed.

I had never seen slow-motion movement before. I had never seen prolonged immobilities, or explosive movements followed by sudden petrification. The actors all had harmonious bodies – not well-articulated bodies – but harmonious ones that were pleasant to watch.

(Decroux, 80th Birthday issue, 39)

The students' harmonious bodies were produced through the study of gymnastics and ballet. The dynamic qualities – slow motion, prolonged immobilities, explosive movements followed by sudden petrification – were doubtless the conscious and unconscious results of Copeau's and his students' efforts to exteriorise the interior conflicts inherent in drama. These same dynamic qualities were also inherent in Copeau's own acting, as well as in that of the key performers of the Théâtre du Vieux Colombier.

Copeau felt the study of masks to be essential to exteriorising the interior conflicts inherent in drama; a certain physical and mental neutrality was found to be the best starting-place. And, although we now take mask training for granted in the schooling of the young actor, it was virtually unheard-of when Copeau developed the technique. Copeau liked to quote Eleonora Duse, one of the most famous actresses of his day, who is supposed to have said that, to save the theatre, the theatre must be destroyed; the actors and actresses must all die of the plague. Copeau's mask exercises were a kind of death to the theatre and the actor as they were then known, but not an end; this death was a necessary precondition of the revival Copeau and his associates envisioned. Jean Dorcy, one of the students at the Ecole du Vieux Colombier, remembers the mask exercises as a deliberate attempt to cut the actor off from the outside world. Then, in that 'night', the actor was to make 'an effort of concentration, to reach a void, a state of un-being. From that moment forward, he will be able to come back to life and behave in a new and truly dramatic way' (Dorcy, 1961, pp. 12, 13).

Copeau felt that the 'void', this 'state of unbeing' followed by a 'coming back to life', was a model of what had to happen to the theatre as a whole, to each individual actor in his or her 'renormalisation' and in each performance. A sometimes painful giving-up of affectation, artifice and *cabotinage* had to precede a rebirth of sincerity, the discovery of the true and fertile source of all theatrical impulse, which would be manifested first in movement, then in inarticulate sound and finally in speech. In a sense, the traditional actor did die of the plague (*cabotinage*) and a new one was born, through the struggle of study and improvisation. Behind the mask, the actor of smiles and grimaces died, and a new corporeal actor was born. In the death of the old paradigm there was an adumbration of the new one. The mask, an object at once primitive and sophisticated, at once a disguise and a revelation, an object of the most ancient and the most modern theatre, was the instrument of rebirth.

Copeau's bare stage was the ideal place, in fact the only place, where this kind of transformation could take place, since the mask imposed an amplitude and a power on movement. It augmented the actor's presence so that the actor alone, regardless of decor and costume, was able to command focus. The kernel of Copeau's teaching is contained in a few words: 'An actor must know how to listen, to answer, to remain motionless, to start a gesture, to follow through with it, come back to motionlessness and silence, with all the shadings and half-tones that these actions imply' (Copeau, 1970, p. 220). This teaching, he found, was best accomplished with the mask.

Michel Saint-Denis, Copeau's nephew, student and later director of the Compagnie des Quinze, who was instrumental in the propagation of Copeau's ideas in England and the United States, observed that masks 'dislike agitation, that they can only be animated by controlled, strong, and utterly simple actions which depend upon the richness of the inner life within the calm and balanced body of the performer'. Mask work, Saint-Denis observed, 'enables the actor to experience, in its most virulent form, the chemistry of acting: at the moment when the actor's feelings are at their height, beneath the mask, the urgent necessity of controlling his physical actions compel him to detachment and lucidity' (Saint-Denis, 1969, pp. 103–4). This juxtaposition of molten interior and cool, classically balanced exterior was a hallmark of Copeau's teaching.

In the Japanese Nō, Copeau found an echo to his own profound interest in the strict demands of form, ensemble acting, the use of masks and corporeal acting. Suzanne Bing, a leading actress in Copeau's theatre and the administrator of the Ecole du Vieux Colombier, worked in summer 1923 with Arthur Waley's and Noel Peri's books on the Nō. Bing and Copeau translated *Kantan* into French from Arthur Waley's *The Nō Plays of Japan*. While trying to be as faithful to the original as possible, Bing and Copeau knew this work would be a reinterpretation and not a reconstruction. Western flute and drum were substituted for Japanese instruments, and the stage movement was necessarily different as the dimensions of the Vieux Colombier stage differed from those of the Nō stage. The French script was notated musically in an attempt to imitate Japanese speech rhythms.

Although a public performance scheduled for March 1924 was cancelled because a lead actor sprained his knee, the play was rehearsed for Copeau, André Gide, the British playwright Harley Granville-Barker and the students of the Ecole du Vieux Colombier. They saw actors wearing masks, or with impassive faces, moving slowly and solemnly, their carefully choreographed movements ending in noble poses, interspersed with slow or lively dances as required. Bing was moved to tears by the emotional intensity of the actors' simple gestures. Granville-Barker, too, was greatly moved and congratulated the students on how much they had been able to accomplish in three years. In ten years, he conjectured, they would be able to do anything. For Copeau it was 'one of the jewels, one of the secret riches of the work of the Vieux Colombier' (1931, p. 100). Michel Saint-Denis remembered it as the 'incomparable summit of our work in Copeau's School/Laboratory' (Rudlin, 1986, p. 49). Decades later Decroux remembered this rehearsal as one of the most beautiful things he had ever seen in the theatre. One could argue that it influenced the whole of Decroux's subsequent work; years later, when he took over the school of the Piccolo Teatro in Milan from Jacques Lecoq, he confided to Lecoq that he hoped to make the students there move like Japanese actors. Gide, alone unmoved, wrote in his journal for 15 January 1931 that it was 'something indefinably strained toward the supernatural in the tone of voice, gestures, and expressions of the actors' (Gide, 1949, p. 139).

Encouraged by the beauty of the Nō, but feeling at a dead end brought about by physical and spiritual exhaustion, Copeau closed his theatre a few months later and adjourned to the country with his school. Copeau's crisis of conscience led him to believe, as many other creators have, that he had done in his life only one or two original things and that the rest of his time had been spent filling in the blanks. After the few brilliant flashes of inspiration and their three-dimensionalisation for a time, who can blame Copeau for not having the heart to institutionalise them? Could he be prophet and priest, research scientist and manufacturer, visionary and bureaucrat? Copeau wanted to move on to the next brilliant moment.

Because of Copeau's exhaustion following so many years of unrelenting labour, and severe financial problems, his active participation in the experiment in the country lasted only five months, although he acted intermittently as the artistic adviser for the Copiaus, a group of former Vieux Colombier actors and students who continued on in Burgundy, until 1929. Copeau's work with the Copiaus moved him further from the text and closer to the actor as the centre of the dramatic event; 'after years of working with actors, I have come to the conviction that the problem of the actor is, at base, a corporeal problem. The actor is standing on the stage' (Rudlin, 1986, p. 93). The Copiaus performed works with slighter texts and more important sequences of dance, mime and celebration than the earlier work done at the Vieux Colombier. After Copeau severed his connection with the Copiaus, they reformed under the direction of Michel Saint-Denis with the name 'La Compagnie des Quinze'. From 1924 until his death in 1949, Copeau worked as a lecturer, teacher, mentor and director of sacred theatre. In the view of his daughter, Marie-Hélène Dasté, this sacred theatre, as realised in Florence and Beaune, came nearest to his highest uncompromised vision of theatre.

Jean Dorcy's description of Copeau the actor is revealing:

> Anyone who has not seen Boverio, Jouvet, and Copeau together in *The Brothers Karamazov* will never, I fear, fully understand the importance of a single word, the density of a gesture, an ominous silence, the expressive force excluding every external device, in short, the significance of style.   (1961, p. 8)

The acting-qualities described here were the ones Copeau found beautiful, the ones he looked for in hiring actors for his theatre, and the ones which he tried to uncover in the students in his school. It is not by accident that these are qualities found in abundance in the Nō theatre, and that would be prominent in the corporeal-mime work of Etienne Decroux.

Kenneth Clark writes in *The Nude* that art is, in its highest form, an expression of religion. When this expression is debased, art becomes entertainment, and then decoration, before it finally disappears. Copeau was a visionary who saw the theatre of entertainment of his day on the verge of falling even further than it already had, into mere decoration. Copeau felt that theatre had to be returned to its sacred state. He thundered like an Old Testament prophet against personal and professional laxity.

One might think, in view of the mystic tone of so much of Copeau's writing, that it was finally souls Copeau was concerned with, not theatre, and that, when his religion became more important than his theatre, the theatre simply fell away, or, at least, ceased to be the quasi-religious obsession it had been before. Marie-Hélène Dasté cautions against drawing conclusions from her father's mid-life conversion to Catholicism. That his religion had an effect on his work, however, cannot be questioned. Even before his conversion, he believed passionately that theatre could unite people of all classes and all nations. Theatre, never a diversion or an amusement for Copeau, was potentially nothing less than the salvation of the individual, society and the world.

Gide conjectured that, because the new authors Copeau needed for his new theatre did not appear, Copeau's 'immense effort remained without any direct relation to the epoch. He was struggling against the epoch, as any good artist must do. But dramatic art has this frightful disadvantage, that it must appeal to the public, count with and on the public' (Gide, 1949, p. 139). This paradox was not to be resolved by Copeau, any more than it would be by Etienne Decroux.

2
Etienne Decroux

Copeau had ignited us so well that those of who left
him took fire with them.   (Etienne Decroux)

On 15 May 1924, when Copeau closed the Théâtre du
Vieux Colombier so that he could devote all of his time
to the school, he decided to take his students to Burgundy
to avoid the distractions of Paris which were antagonistic
to his work. Among those students who were invited to
go to the country was one Etienne Decroux – included, it
was once conjectured, not so much because he was a
promising student (which he no doubt was) but because
he had been an apprentice butcher and the school was felt
to need a person with those qualifications. About fifteen
people in all went with Copeau to Morteuil in 1924.
Madame Chennevière, wife of the poet and teacher,
accompanied her husband and acted as mistress of the
house and director of the kitchen. Madame Dasté remembers Decroux's bare torso as he deftly cut the meat on a

marble slab in the kitchen, his economical gestures already those of a mime. These economical gestures of the working person were one of the primary influences on Decroux's art; he was often heard to say that working people perform the simplest, most efficient and least tiring movements, as they have to conserve their energy in order to make it through their long days. Copeau too had remarked upon working people's economy of gesture. 'That comes from their really doing something, that they do what they do and do it well, knowing the reason, absorbing themselves in it' (Rudlin, 1986, p. 45).

As a child, Decroux seems to have had a particularly close relationship with his father. There cannot have been too many people in their working-class neighbourhood who read poetry aloud to their children, or visited a family of Italian sculptors. His father took the young boy every Monday to a *café-concert*, a type of variety music-hall. It was there that Decroux first saw the last gasps of nine-teenth-century pantomime. Decroux's father, a construction worker, built with his own hands their house in Boulogne-Billancourt, the one in which Decroux still lives. He was as interested in politics as he was in construction techniques, and held long discussions with his son about justice.

Until he was twenty-five, Etienne Decroux worked in construction, but he had also been a painter, a plumber, a mason, a tile-setter, a butcher, a navvy, a docker, a coach-repairer, a dish-washer, a hospital attendant and a farm worker. His discussions with his father on the nature of justice and injustice led him to strong political convictions; yet, for one of humble origins, with an *accent du faubourg*, and in a world where artificially amplified sound had yet to be invented, diction lessons would be necessary for an aspiring politician. One day on the street, the young Decroux saw a sign announcing diction classes at the Ecole du Vieux Colombier. He enrolled in 1923.

While Copeau had come to the theatre from literature, above the theatre of his day, Decroux came to it from the working classes, from below, and each brought fresh insights from the other métier. The muscular young Decroux, dressed in the suit, hat and large bow tie of the early militant socialists, impressed his fellow students with his verbosity, and was promptly nicknamed the Orator. Even then he was quick to point out the irreconcilable difference between art, the publicity-seeker, and politics, the saint.

Decroux responded wholeheartedly to Copeau's teaching. Copeau's devotion to the theatre, his purism, inspired the idealistic Decroux. Years later Decroux was to acknowledge often and readily that he would never have done what he had had it not been for the exercises he witnessed, the improvisations with inexpressive masks, at the Ecole du Vieux Colombier. In the commencement exercises for the A-section students, Decroux saw the potential for corporeal mime, revealed to him in embryonic form in these masked exercises. He became sure that it was an art which could only be degraded, at least at its earliest stage of development, by the addition of the spoken word, and that it was an art which could become infinitely superior to traditional theatre as it was then practised. When the first group of students from the Ecole du Vieux Colombier in Burgundy dispersed after five months, Decroux went to work in Paris first with Gaston Baty, and then with Louis Jouvet, actors trained by Copeau. Decroux felt in Jouvet's acting 'the beginnings of, a taste for, the marionette . . . a certain way of turning the head, of using his neck, a certain way of taking his place on the stage. One sensed in him the articulated man.' While elements in Decroux's synthesis came from Copeau's teaching, Decroux said that 'the style came to me with Jouvet' (Decroux, 1978, p. 14).

Decroux stayed with Jouvet for the 1925 season, then joined Charles Dullin's troupe at the Théâtre de l'Atelier in Montmartre in 1926, where he stayed until 1934 as an actor in the troupe and mime-teacher in the school. Dullin was, like Baty and Jouvet, formerly of Copeau's troupe. Decroux admits to having been formed by Dullin, who took him in a rudimentary state and gave him a sense of good taste, a sense of measure and of passion in his acting. Decroux admired Dullin's acting, and found him exciting to work with. A photograph of Charles Dullin in *Les Frères Karamazov* at the Théâtre des Arts in Paris in 1911 gives some indication of why Decroux was so enthusiastic. The intensity of Dullin's acting is evident in the whole body. Several hallmarks of the technique that would later be known as corporeal mime can be seen in it. The weight is thrust forward onto one leg: a plumb-line dropped from the centre of the trunk would cut the ankle, showing a forward gravity that is one kind of counterweight. The diagonal line from top of head to tip of left foot would be called a 'heroic diagonal' by art historian Kenneth Clark; this is the diagonal Decroux noticed as typical of statues which date from the period of the French Revolution as well as other periods of political and physical engagement. Decroux saw in it the line of a body which risks itself. The independent and clear movement of the eyes adds to the crispness and clarity of line. The stance is an actor's choice, not chance. This choice is infused with a dynamic; it is not just a pretty statue. We can see in this photo what moved the young Decroux as well as the more experienced Copeau to enthusiastic praise of Dullin's acting.

Dullin attributed his acting-style to his observation of

the last of the melodrama actors, who were still performing with expressive ardour in the local theatres when he was a young actor. These actors were called 'board burners' for their charismatic way of performing. Both Jouvet and Dullin had consciously absorbed something of the acting-style of melodrama actors, or 'crabs' as they were called, since they walked sideways so as never to turn their backs to the audience. Was it because Copeau's first experiences at the theatre were melodramas on the Boulevard du Temple that he admired their work? It is ironic that this influence on Decroux's modern mime had originally come from nineteenth-century pantomime, as pantomime became melodrama when texts and songs were added; modern mime's one real connection with the outworn paradigm it replaced is via the hybrid of melodrama.

In the 1920s the young Decroux and his contemporaries in other arts rebelled with a vengeance against the nine-teenth-century paradigms. They felt that it was essential not only artistically, but morally, spiritually and politically as well, to show their disdain for the middle class, the routine, the *status quo*. Modern art was not a decoration for these young rebels, a mere amusement; it was a way of life, a battle cry, a *raison d'être*. To be alive was to be socialist–anarchist, surrealist, cubist, vegetarian, nudist, an advocate of free love. As a young man with long hair and wearing sandals, Decroux was spat upon and shouted at by people on the street who were critical of these attitudes.

Paris was a veritable battleground of conflicting styles, movements and manifestos in the first quarter of the twentieth century; the opening shot of this chaotic struggle was fired in 1896 with the first performance of Alfred Jarry's *Ubu Roi*. The Futurist Manifesto was published in 1909. In 1913 Valentine de Saint-Point presented a futurist combination of poems, dance and projections to music by Debussy and Satie. In 1914 Giacomo Balla presented his *Macchina tipografica* in a private performance for Diaghilev. Each of twelve performers impersonated a single part of a complicated printing-press, reproducing both sound and movement in front of a curtain on which had been painted the word 'tipografica'. Inspired by Craig's essay on the super-marionette, futurists created marionettes in various sizes and staged performances with them exclusively, as well as in concert with human performers. Manifestos entitled 'Futurist Synthetic Theatre', 'Futurist Pantomime', and 'Futurist Dance' were published, and performances by Nijinsky, Isadora Duncan and Loie Fuller had tremendous effect on the artists in Paris.

Beginning in 1928, Decroux started work with young people to form a mime troupe. They proved inconstant, so he created *La Vie primitive* with his wife Suzanne, whom he married in 1930, and they performed it at the Salle Lancry in Paris on 13 June 1931. Primitive life is not a surprising choice of subject matter for a young artist in the 1930s. Modernism owes much to the primitive works that began to be seen in Europe in the early decades of this century. An exhibition entitled 'Primitivism in Twentieth Century Art', organised by the Museum of Modern Art in New York, was shown in major American cities in 1985. The exhibition attempted to test the thesis that tribal art of Africa and the South Seas had a great influence on the founders of modern art. Just as the work of Picasso, Matisse, Miró, Gauguin and Giacometti was radically changed by their contact with such art, so Decroux, Artaud and Barrault were deeply influenced by the performances of Balinese and Cambodian dancers on their infrequent visits to Paris. Decroux was influenced not only in his choice of subject matter, but in movement qualities as well, as he incorporated certain articulated movements derived from Cambodian dance into his technique, a technique already influenced by the Nō play. What cubism was for Picasso, corporeal mime was for Decroux.

In 1931 Jean-Louis Barrault came to the Théâtre de l'Atelier for lessons, and there the twenty-year-old Barrault met Decroux, then a member of Dullin's troupe. Barrault remembers Decroux as an eccentric who stylised his roles to the point of dancing them, and whose friends spoke of him with a little sidelong smile. Decroux, at that time a 'puritan revolutionary' who 'cultivated the more-than-perfect' (Barrault, 1951, pp. 21, 23), was looking for people to continue the corporeal work he had begun at the Vieux Colombier. Barrault was young and enthusiastic, and was easily won over; he became Decroux's first real pupil, his disciple. Any account of Decroux's life at this period, and any account of the beginnings of corporeal mime, finds Barrault's story inextricably mixed with Decroux's, as for two years they were inseparable: nudists, vegetarians, 'accomplices in search of a new mime' (Barrault, 1972, p. 72). The story of those two years has been often told: Decroux sat and wrote as Barrault improvised – Decroux the analytical codifier, the reasoner; Barrault intuitive, creative and mystical. At the end of two years, they performed their *Combat antique* for Dullin. Dullin, who encouraged their work but was not without scepticism, was completely won over by their performance, which he felt had reached the technical perfection of Japanese actors. Despite the seeming hostility of Decroux and Barrault's colleagues at the Atelier, whose card games were disturbed by the two innovators as they bounded about the corridors and rehearsal halls of the theatre, and despite Dullin's slight scepticism, the Atelier was in fact one of the most progressive theatres in Paris at that time, and one of the few where this kind of experiment would have been tolerated at all. Dullin embraced the idea of the theatre as a laboratory for dramatic experiments, and, like that of his mentor, Copeau, his theatre included a school.

The fervour of those two years of white-hot creativity and discovery was not to endure, since Barrault noticed what most of Decroux's students have remarked since: Decroux's passion for his art was uncompromising, and the rigour of his devotion was finally oppressive for everyone except Decroux himself. Decroux's rigour extended beyond the classroom and onto the stage, where, if a performance was not going as well as he wanted, he would stop it, and even insult the audience if they laughed inappropriately and uncomprehendingly at his experimental work.

Whereas Copeau had a vision of theatre as a whole, a whole which included text, movement and decor (albeit in a limited way), he devised training-exercises which separated movement from speech so that it could be more carefully studied. From these pedagogical exercises, modern mime was born. These movement exercises collided with the classicist, purist temperament of Decroux, and from that collision corporeal mime came into being. Yet, contrary to what many believe, Decroux never intended silent corporeal mime to exist for ever as an independent art.

Decroux was in fact a busy actor on stage, screen and radio from 1925 until 1945. He played over sixty-five roles in works by Aristophanes, Ruzzante, Shakespeare, Ben Jonson, Molière, Tolstoy, Strindberg, Pirandello, Marcel Achard and Jules Romains. His directors were, among others, Copeau, Gaston Baty, Jouvet, Dullin, Artaud and Marcel Herrand. He performed in more than thirty films, often directed by Jacques Prévert and Marcel Carné, including *Les Enfants du paradis*. And, while he did this to earn his living, he continued to create, evolve and nurture corporeal mime.

His public mime performances, however, were few. His love of perfection made him so demanding, both of himself and his actors on one hand, and of his audience (most of whom were seeing modern mime for the first time) on the other, that he finally wanted to perform for only two or three people, since he felt that people were freer to see something new in smaller groups.

In 1938 Decroux performed one hundred times in his dining-room for audiences of two or three. In 1940, as he continued to polish the line and rhythm of his pieces *La Machine*, *Le Menuisier*, *La Lessive* and *Les Marches de personage sur place*, he performed another hundred times for audiences of three and four. In 1941 Decroux opened his school, and gave a private performance of *Camping* at the Comédie des Champs-Elysées. In 1942 he and his students performed *Chirurgie esthétique*, *Dernière conquête* and *Passage des hommes sur la terre* about one hundred times, in a large dining-room, for audiences of from five to ten persons.

As one reads through the newspaper clippings of reviews from these years, one frequently comes across phrases such as 'magnificent ardour' describing the way Decroux and his students approached their work. Decroux is called a 'zealot of mime' and 'a curious man, with fixed and fevered eyes . . . a high priest'. Decroux's actors were seen as, for example, the 'priestess of a mysterious cult' and 'a young Egyptian god, participating in the rites of this strange religion'. One of the most vivid of these articles concludes with the observation, 'Etienne Decroux, who resembles a prehistoric man, plays his body as one plays a violin.'

In spring 1942 Gaston Baty, with whom Decroux had worked when he first left Copeau, wrote an open letter to a newspaper in which he charged Decroux with 'trying to isolate from the dramatic process the mimetic element, which he likes for its own sake' and in so doing 'he is once more mutilating the major art for the benefit of a manifestation which is, in spite of everything, minor. Such an amputation does not even offer us a body from which a limb has been severed, but instead a limb from which the body has been severed.' Decroux's reply to Baty, important enough to Decroux for him to include it in his *Words on Mime*, begins with his now famous statement, 'I think an art is all the richer for being poor in means.' Then, in his spare, evocative and aphoristic style he develops, more like a poem than an essay on aesthetics, his reply. His main argument is that 'Orthodox theatre, scarcely being an art [since it "suggests the thing by the thing itself"] has little chance of being complete.' And he sums up by writing, 'for art to be, the idea of one thing must be given by another thing. Hence this paradox; an art is complete only if it is partial.' Decroux closes by quoting Baudelaire – 'les parfums, les couleurs et les sons se répondent' – and George Chennevière: 'le monde est en entier présent dans chaque object' (Decroux, 1985, pp. 28–30).

Here Decroux seems fanatically against the mixing of speech or music with mime. Yet Decroux himself is an accomplished orator, storyteller and actor. His contemporaries recognised that his knowledge of metrics, phonetics and pronunciation as well as literature and prosody was as great as his ability in mime. Except in a few rare cases, where he has combined mime with poetry readings for comic effect, Decroux has kept his two great abilities separated. And, no matter how vehemently he was to argue for separation of speech and movement, he knew that one day a synthesis was inevitable. In *Words on Mime* he advocates banning ordinary speech from the theatre for a *limited period* (thirty years), or until the actor had taken charge in his own house. Vocal sound would be proscribed altogether for a period of twenty years, after which the voice, and finally speech, would gradually reappear, but controlled by the actor, used only when necessary and not out of laziness or lack of inventive ability. Decroux offered this cure for a theatre which he thought was 'suffocating under a heap of rubble':

1. For a period of thirty years, the proscription of every alien art. We shall replace the drawing-room setting with the setting of the theatre itself, our intention being solely to provide a background for all imaginable actions.
2. For the first ten years of this thirty year period: the proscription of any elevation on stage, such as stools, staircases, terraces, balconies, etc. The actor will have to give the impression that he is higher and his partner lower, even when in reality they are side by side. Later, the authorisation of certain forms of elevation on condition that they create even greater difficulties for the actor.
3. For the first twenty years of this thirty year period: the proscription of any vocal sound. Then the acceptance of inarticulate cries for five years.

   Finally, words are accepted for the last five years of the thirty year period, but invented by the actor.

4. After this period of war: stability. Plays shall be composed in the following order:

   A. Rough outline of the written action serving as a basis for work.
   B. The actor miming his action, then accompanying it with inarticulate sounds, then improvising his text.
   C. Introduction of a dramaturge to translate the text into choice language, without adding a word.
   D. Reappearance of alien arts, but practised by the actors. And when the actor is master in his own home he shall see to the employment of dancers, singers and musicians for the indispensable and well-defined tasks. And then we shall see on the poster: 'text arranged by Mr Secondo'.

   (Decroux, 1985, pp. 26–7)

Decroux wrote this in 1931, the same year that the Compagnie des Quinze presented for a brief period two works by André Obey, *Noé* and *Le Viol*, at the Vieux Colombier. The programme notes identified the productions as 'the first fruits of a close collaboration between a dramatist and a company of players'. The note goes on to explain that Obey could not have written these plays without having seen Copeau's work, as they demanded actors as highly trained in mime as in speech (Rudlin, 1986, p. 30).

Whereas Gide speculated that Copeau's efforts were frustrated by the lack of authors writing for the new theatre, Decroux put the responsibility squarely on the new actor for the creation of a new text and a new theatre. Fifty years after Decroux wrote this manifesto, post-modern performers would at last begin to perform pieces they had created and devised themselves. If Decroux only offered poetry mixed with mime for comic effect, he did often throughout his career offer readings from his favourite poets – among them Victor Hugo, Baudelaire and Verhaeren, all poets Copeau had included in his poetry-readings at the Théâtre du Vieux Colombier. Sounds, in the form of audible breathing, the pounding of heels, the click of tongue against the roof of the mouth or against teeth, seem always to have been a part of Decroux's mime performances. From the beginning, perhaps because the masked exercises at the Vieux Colombier were more often than not accompanied by vocal sounds and body percussion (while in Burgundy, Copeau's associates had experimented with *grummelotage* or 'the music of meaning'), Decroux's mime, too, has almost invariably been so accompanied. These sounds indicate shock, resonance, reverberation and numerous other kinds of causality that occur in corporeal mime.

While never having had the time to work on it as a separate art, Decroux has often spoken of vocal mime as a rich field for exploration. Such mime would take the sighs and cries naturally emitted in the course of movement and develop them into a highly expressive art. And, while he may never have explored this area formally, Decroux's teaching and performance have seldom been without a vocal component. Like the Canadian pianist Glenn Gould, who found it almost impossible to play the piano without singing or making grunting noises, because for him the music and the sounds he uttered were all coming from the same place, so Decroux early on recognised that sound and movement came from the same source, and could be separated only in theory. In theory, Decroux proposed the prohibition of any vocal sound from the theatre for twenty years as part of his programme for renewing the theatre; in practice, he found it difficult to eliminate sounds from his own work for even twenty minutes.

In October 1942 Decroux gave public performances at the Salon d'Automne and at the Théâtre des Ambassadeurs. In 1943 he and Barrault performed in the now legendary film *Les Enfants du paradis*. In 1944 Decroux and some of his students gave private showings for ten to fifty people in the small hall of the Foyer des Beaux Arts, and in 1945 Decroux and Barrault performed their *Combat antique* as part of *Antony and Cleopatra* at the Comédie Française.

One of the most important mime events of this period was the performance of 27 June 1945 at the Maison de la Chimie in Paris. More than 1000 spectators attended a performance of coporeal mime given by Decroux, Barrault and Eliane Guyon with Jean Dorcy as master of ceremonies and Gordon Craig as guest of honour. Describing in a newspaper article what took place, Jean Dorcy gives us a coherent definition of corporeal mime:

> With corporeal mime, we no longer read known forms, we decode, reassemble, and appreciate according to our knowledge and our emotional state: the passive observer becomes active. Could one dream of a more fecund meeting of actor and audience?
>
> (Dorcy, unidentified Paris newspaper clipping, 1945)

Dorcy's choice of the world 'decode' must not be understood to mean that Decroux's mime was of the guessing-game variety. Quite to the contrary: Decroux has always detested that kind of illusionistic play which casts the audience in the role of translator, trying to interpret the performer's signals. Decroux, instead, proceeded by analogy and by metaphor. He said that when

he saw one person stand up, he saw humanity raise itself.
Dorcy's article continues:

> Let us understand that the corporeal mime wants a bare
> stage, nude actors, and no variation in lighting. For
> once, the theatre is no longer a cross-roads of all the
> arts, but the triumph of one art only: that of the body
> in motion.

This kind of purity comes directly from the doctrines of
Copeau, taken one or two steps further, and clearly
identifies Decroux's work as modernist, contemporaneous
with the work of Mondrian, Brancusi and others who liked
to reduce things to their essence.

The express purpose of the performance, according to
the programme book, was to show up the doctrinal links
from Craig to Copeau, from Copeau to Decroux, from
Decroux to Barrault, evoking along the way the work of
Appia. The programme consisted of eight pieces. The
first, entitled *Evocation d'actions matérielles*, consisted of
three parts: *Le Menuisier*, *La Lessive* and *La Machine*.
Le Menuisier and *La Lessive* were evocations through
simplification and amplification of the work performed by
an individual: in the first, of sawing, planing, hammering
and other actions associated with carpentry; in the second,
washing, rinsing, wringing, hanging out to dry and mending
laundry. Decroux chose his title well; he did indeed mean
evocation rather than depiction or reproduction. An
audience member might not, without the title, have any
more notion that Decroux had begun with these actions
than an observer of a cubist painting would, without the
title, be able to identify the subject of the painter's work.
These corporeal-mime studies are, however, like the best
cubist painting, the result of careful study of the object or

action in nature before the transposition into art. I worked with Decroux almost every day from 1968 until 1972 to learn *Le Mensuisier* and *La Lessive*. The rehearsals were difficult and consisted of trying to reproduce exact and usually uncomfortable positions succeeding each other rapidly. Each second of the approximately seven minutes required to perform each piece was exactly choreographed in terms of line, dynamic quality, facial expression, breath and weight, and not a single gesture or placement of head, hands or feet was arbitrary. Everything was the result of choice, and the choice was usually made in relation to the physical reality of the action being depicted. The result, however, was as far from the charming and romantic pantomime of the nineteenth century as the paintings of Picasso are from the work of nineteenth-century salon artists.

The third part of the first piece was entitled *La Machine*. The machine is not an unusual subject in the graphic arts, theatre, dance and mime in these years of the futurists and a society radically changed by machines and desperately trying to come to terms with them. This composition, like almost all Decroux's mime pieces, had its genesis in exercises performed at the Ecole du Vieux Colombier and continually reworked since. For some fifty years Decroux spent some part of every day creating or reconstructing mime pieces.

This suite of what was basically a study of work carried out by both humans and machines was followed in the programme by *Une Étude du 'contrepoids'*, performed by students of Decroux's school. Decroux taught counter-weight studies for years; they consisted of a careful analysis of what the body did to push, pull or otherwise displace objects of varying weights. Most spectators found this the weakest part of the programme, as the young students were not yet stage-worthy, and the material was the nearest thing in the programme to training-exercises.

Decroux then performed *Le Boxer*, *Le Lutteur*, *Le Bureaucrate* and *Quelques passants*. He always had a penchant for detecting and satirising affectation, and, while the boxer and wrestler were probably portrayed in a more abstract and noble way, concentrating on the dynamics of sports movements, Decroux's sharp wit probably delighted in skewering and deflating an affectation or two in the bureaucrat or the passers-by.

This suite was followed by a symbolist mime chorus. As a young man, Decroux had participated enthusiastically in the speaking choruses of the radical socialists. The idea of many voices blending together to articulate a single idea was one that always exercised a strong control over Decroux's imagination. On this occasion the chorus consisted of only three actors (Decroux, Barrault and Eliane Guyon), who performed *Le Passage des hommes sur la terre*. This piece, revived in the 1950s for Decroux's New York company, is a panoramic evocation of famine, mass movements of population, revolution and finally peace. As such, there is no story-line or attempt at characterisation, but instead an evocative, symbolic collage which gives rise to diffuse yet intense feelings in the spectator.

The next piece in the programme was a work-in-progress entitled *Matériaux d'une pièce biblique*, subtitled *Figures juxtaposées sans lien dramatique*, performed by Decroux and Eliane Guyon. Decroux's aversion to traditional plot-line shows up in every one of the pieces in this programme, to the extent of its being a part of the title of this piece (*sans lien dramatique*: 'without dramatic relationship').

Jean-Louis Barrault performed his famous horse-taming sequence next, an extract from his 1935 production of

Autour d'une mère (an adaptation of William Faulkner's *As I Lay Dying*, and discussed in the next chapter). This was followed by *Statuaire mobile (avec visage couvert)*. This consisted of *Maladie–agonie–mort,* another piece derived from *Autour d'une mère,* and *Différence entre admiration–adoration–vénération.* The performance part of the evening drew to a climax with a performance of *Combat antique* by Decroux and Barrault.

The evening ended with a lecture on the differences between pantomime and corporeal mime. Dorcy and others found this inappropriate, following as it did the livelier parts of the programme. It was, however, very much like Decroux the orator, the student of French literature, to want to provide a commentary, an explication of the 'text' the audience had just seen. The programme that evening was heralded by Gordon Craig in his often reprinted and cited 'Enfin un créateur au théâtre', an article in which Craig confidently places Decroux in the forefront of post-war European theatre.

In 1946 Decroux and his students presented *L'Usine, Les Arbres* and *L'Esprit malin* at the Théâtre d'Iéna in Paris. In the years that followed, Decroux and a small company toured Belgium, Switzerland, Holland, Israel and England as well as giving performances in Paris. Among the new works created during this period are *Petits soldats*, *Prise de contact*, *Jeu de dames* and *Soirée*.

In October 1957 Decroux went on a long teaching, lecture and performance tour of the United States. He founded a school in New York which gave birth to a company of American actors who performed with him in New York at the Kaufmann Concert Hall, Carnegie Hall and the Cricket Theatre. At this time he also performed solo lecture–demonstrations and taught short workshops at various universities around the United States, among

1. Jean-Louis Barrault and Marie-Hélène Dasté in *Christophe Colombe*. Photograph © Studio Bernand.

2. (*left*) Jean-Louis Barrault in the early days of his film career. Unattributed photograph.

4. Etienne Decroux in his study, Paris, 1953. Photograph © Etienne
Bertrand Weill.

5. Edward Gordon Craig visiting Etienne Decroux's school, Paris, 1947. From left to right: Roger Demar, unidentified, M. Soussan, Marcel Marceau, Etienne Decroux, Gordon Craig and his daughter, Eliane Guyon,

6. (*left*) Etienne Decroux demonstrating an exercise in his Paris school, 1975. Photograph © Christian Mattis Schmocker.

7. (*right*) Etienne Decroux, Paris, 1975. Photograph © Christian Mattis Schmocker.

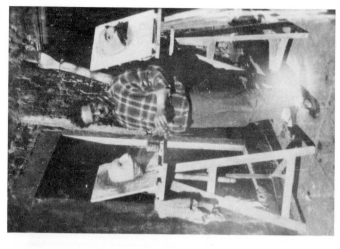

8. (*left*) Etienne Decroux in 'Sport', 1948. Photograph © Etienne Bertrand Weill.

10. Jacques Copeau in the role of Plébère in *L'Illusion*, a play created by Copeau for the Copiaus, at Pernand-Vergelesses in 1926. Photograph © M.H. Dasté.

11. The Vieux Colombier company performing *Les Fourberies de Scapin* outdoors in the Place St Sulpice, Paris, c. 1920. Photograph © M.H. Dasté.

12. Director, teacher, actor and theatre visionary Jacques Copeau.
Photograph © French Embassy Press and Information Division,
N.Y.C.

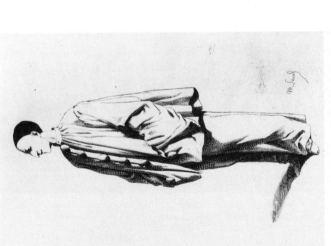

13. Deburau as Pierrot by Maurice Sand. © Bibliothèque de l'Arsenal, Paris.

14. Pierrot with long sleeves by Maurice Sand. © Bibliothèque de l'Arsenal, Paris.

15. Ink drawing of Jean-Gaspard Deburau by Michael Tomek, based on lithographs in the Bibliothèque de l'Arsenal. © Mime Journal.

16. French mime Marcel Marceau teaching class. Photograph ©
Rebecca Knight.

17. French mime Marcel Marceau as Bip. Unattributed photograph.

18. Marcel Marceau in performance. Photograph © Gapihan.

19. Jacques Lecoq teaching with the help of leather masks by Amleto Sartori. Photograph © *The Glasgow Herald*.

20. Jacques Lecoq. Photograph © Patrick Lecoq.

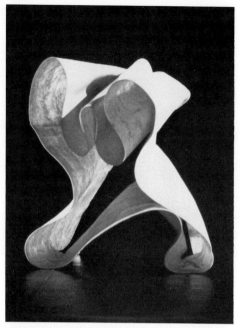

21. A Mummenschanz full-body mask from their second show.
Photograph © Christian Altorfer.

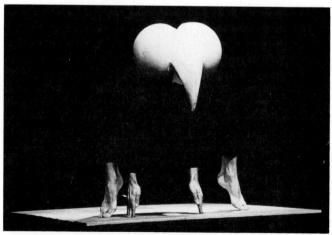

22. A moment from the first Mummenschanz show. Photograph ©
Gapihan.

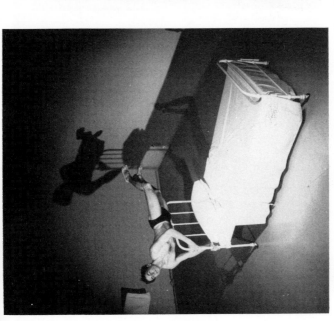

23. (*left*) Gilles Maheu in 'L'Homme rouge'. Photograph © Yves Dubé.

24. (*right*) Daniel Stein in 'Inclined to Agree'. Photograph Paul Martens, © Winnipeg International Mime Festival.

25. (*left*) Steven Wasson and Corinne Soum in 'La Croisade'. Unattributed photograph.

them Tufts in Medford, Mass. and Baylor in Waco, Texas. The repertoire of his New York company included revivals of some of the works he had produced before in Europe, among them *The Factory* (*L'Usine*) and *Trees* (*Les Arbres*), certain of Decroux's solo pieces, and a new duet entitled *The Statue*, with Decroux playing the sculptor. Among the solo works Decroux performed for thunderstruck and uncomprehending audiences (Henry Hewes understood some of the work; among the critics only Eric Bentley really 'got' it) was Decroux's signature piece, *The Carpenter* (*Le Menuisier*).

The struggle of the manual labourer against gravity, fatigue, the weight and resistance of material objects and his own inertia led Decroux to emulate the example in *Emile*, where Rousseau made his ideal son a carpenter. The carpenter, an appropriate symbol for Decroux in his artistic struggle, is like the corporeal mime who struggles first with his own thought; then with matter – the inertia of his own body, wood, rock, earth; then with one other person; then with the group. This progression, often cited by Decroux in his teaching, provides a convenient classification for most of the works he created. While far from a complete inventory of Decroux's work, the above description suggests the variety and texture of his *oeuvre*. He continued creating works with his students in his basement school in Paris until well into his eighties, in the 1980s.

Decroux spent five years in New York, and when he returned to Paris took up residence in what had been his father's house in an inner suburb of Paris, where his school remained until 1986. After New York, Decroux's interest in performing, never strong, diminished even further until it almost dissappeared. He continued to perform daily in class, but his interest in placing himself or his students before uninitiated audiences was slight or non-existent. The little school in the basement of his house flourished during these years, producing a succession of performers and teachers for many parts of the world. The number of students enrolled varied from as few as six or eight to as many as 100 in three separate classes each day. Through relative success and almost complete obscurity, Decroux, like Copeau before him, has remained firmly wedded to his ideals.

Decroux's name conjures up many varied images. As one of the central figures in the development of modern mime, everyone in the field has heard of him, and many more have studied briefly with him during his fifty years of teaching. But, because of his unusual aversion to performing, few, even among the specialists, have seen him perform or have seen performances directed by him. For the general public, even now, mime is synonymous with the image popularised by Marcel Marceau; the name Etienne Decroux has virtually no public recognition.

Decroux's obscurity is self-perpetrating. A recently published scholarly study of modern mime, including a chapter on Etienne Decroux, was written by a person who admitted in conversation with me to never having seen a single work choreographed or performed by Decroux, either in performance or on film. That same person had never taken a single lesson with Decroux and never interviewed him. It was with some difficulty that I convinced this person to try to see the teaching and perform-ances of some of the artists who had been trained by Decroux. What scholar could write a chapter on a poet whose works he had never read, or on a painter whose paintings he had never seen, even in reproduction, or on a composer whose compositions he had never studied in depth?

Part of the difficulty of understanding Decroux's work stems from the way it developed and changed over fifty years. One era included illusionistic pantomime; the most brilliant student from that period was Marcel Marceau. For a time Decroux's only claim to renown was as a teacher of Marceau and Barrault; consequently some have persisted in describing Decroux as an illusionistic pantomime artist, even though he worked for only a brief time in this style.

Decroux's work, like Picasso's, shows a large number of different styles and approaches over a long career. Just as cubism was a significant, and in different forms, recurrent approach for Picasso, so it has been for Decroux. But it is only one of the approaches Decroux has taken. Whereas with Picasso one can easily see the differences in style when his paintings are hung side by side in a museum, Decroux's compositions have for the most part been written on air, ephemeral and not easily given to comparison or analysis, a problem which is compounded as their audience has been so small over the years.

Just as Decroux's earlier teaching sparked off the careers of Marceau and Barrault, so his later, more abstract work did the same for the French soloist Yves Lebreton, and the directors of the Théâtre du Mouvement, Claire Heggen and Yves Marc; the Franco-American couples Corinne Soum and Steve Wasson, and Veera Wibaux and Bert Houle; the Belgian director Jan Ruts, of Pyramide op de Punt; the Dutch directors Willie Spoor and Frits Vogels; the Canadians Denise Boulanger and Jean Asselin (Omnibus), Gilles Maheu (Carbonne 14), George Molnar and Giuseppe Condello; the Americans Leonard Pitt, Jan Munroe, Daniel Stein, Marguerite Mathews (Pontine), Dulcinea Langfelder, Kari Margolis and Tony Brown (The Adaptors); William Fisher; and others. This diverse group has as its primary unifying characteristic a similar basis in training and a similar post-modern thrust in performance.

Decroux's belief in the importance of technical training has been viewed by some theatre practitioners as dangerously sterilising. His answer has been to compare mime study to technical study in music or dance; it is accepted that great dancers and musicians are not hampered by technique, but freed by it for expression. Not everyone has seen this point as clearly as Eugenio Barba: 'the actor who works within a network of codified rules has a greater liberty than he who – like the Occidental actor – is a prisoner of arbitrariness and an absence of rules'. Barba goes on to compare Decroux's teachings to those of Oriental techniques.

> in the same way that a Kabuki actor can ignore the best 'secrets' of Noh, it is symptomatic that Etienne Decroux, perhaps the only European master to have elaborated a system of rules comparable to that of an Oriental tradition, seeks to transmit to his students the same rigorous closedness to theatre forms different from his own.   (Barba, 1982, p. 6)

One of the best, and most recent spokesmen in the old form-*versus*-content debate is Jerzy Grotowski, from whom Barba doubtless acquired some of his taste for highly structured work that permits spontaneity. Grotowski has written,

> It is the true lesson of the sacred theatre; whether we speak of the medieval European drama, the Balinese or the Indian Kathakali: this knowledge that spontaneity and discipline, far from weakening each other, mutually reinforce themselves; that what is elementary feeds what

is constructed and vice versa, to become the real source of a kind of acting that glows. This lesson was neither understood by Stanislavski, who let natural impulses dominate, nor by Brecht, who gave too much emphasis to the construction of a role.

(Grotowski, 1968, p. 121)

Decroux wrote the following as a programme note for a series of lectures he gave in Ghent, Belgium, in 1972:

[My teaching] is the breaking apart of the natural and the composition of the ideal. That is chemistry's method, also painting's, the method of all the fine arts, with the exception of the actor's art – and especially music, the most technical art on the one hand and the most faithful representation of the movement of the soul on the other. We would like, therefore, for the mime's body to be to the mime as the keyboard is to the pianist. As for the designs which the whole body must be able to accomplish, or each part of it, or each group of parts, they proceed from the geometric spirit. . . . If it is obvious for everyone that, in music, technique neither paralyses nor sterilises inspiration but, on the contrary, aids its birth, excites it, gives ceremonial dress, one none the less sees the actor's art differently.

Decroux, however, does *not* see the actor's art differently; he believes that mime is first of all a serious art and only secondarily a comic one. Painting, sculpture, dance and drama are all primarily serious and only secondarily, if at all, funny. For some reason mime is linked in the popular mind with comedy, while Decroux has stressed the more sublime and noble aspects of the art.

A musical scale has long existed; a colour wheel and

grey scale have long been a part of the visual artist's standard equipment. Dance has had a codified basis for centuries, but it took Etienne Decroux to carve out a specific mime scale, or series of scales, for the body. These scales – inclinations of head, hammer (head plus neck), bust (head plus neck plus chest), torso (head plus neck plus chest plus waist), trunk (head plus neck plus chest plus waist plus pelvis), with a conform or contrary axle, and so on and so forth – are just the beginning of a technique that includes counterweights (physical and moral), figures of style, figures of sport, walks, arm and hand techniques, mobile statuary, and so on.

Research has always taken precedence over performance for Decroux. From necessity, his performance material has usually been drawn from work in the classroom, since the only way for Decroux to obtain actors capable of realising his concepts was to train them. Just as there were no Graham dancers before Martha Graham trained them, so there were no corporeal mimes before Decroux taught them. Most dancers lacked the requisite sense of weight, or the minute articulations necessary for corporeal mime. Some speaking actors had the necessary sense of drama and a taste for immobility, but lacked specific physical training in corporeal mime.

Critics have often found the scent of the schoolroom too strong in Decroux's performance work. Some have called his presentations academic, dogmatic, purist and esoteric. Decroux has dismissed these criticisms with the argument that eyes accustomed to lighter, more entertaining fare could not see the depth and weight of what he was attempting.

Gordon Craig, in reviewing the programme of 27 June 1945, made some clear and often quoted observations on the importance of what he saw. In this article, reprinted in the January 1980 issue of *Empreintes*, Craig said that in Decroux's performance he had witnessed the 'creation of an alphabet – an ABC of mime'. Such statements depicting Decroux as a 'grammarian of mime' have encouraged the literal-minded to imagine that Decroux substituted movements for words, when his achievement was, quite to the contrary, to give movements a primacy of their own, independent of words. In this he stands in direct contrast to the nineteenth-century Pierrot, whose movements did in fact replace forbidden words.

3
Jean-Louis Barrault

Barrault was born a dancer, made himself into a great
mime, and finally delighted in being a dramatic actor.
(Jean Dorcy)

We are not one, but three.   (Jean-Louis Barrault)

The ugly child with large head and bowed legs who needed
eighteen months to learn to walk would later be noted for
his exceptional beauty and grace in movement. His father
died when he was a youngster, and he says he has spent
his life 'looking for the Father' (Barrault, 1972, p. 29).
Barrault especially like mathematics, sometimes solved
problems while dreaming, and loved to realise two-dimen-
sional drawings three-dimensionally. Like Decroux, he
knew manual labour, having worked as a shepherd, a
grape-grower, a harvester and a flower-salesman. Barrault
studied briefly at the Ecole du Louvre, but his attempts
at painting were unsuccessful. It was a letter he sent to

Charles Dullin at the Théâtre de l'Atelier that found him his vocation. Although Barrault had dreamed of acting, he had been to the theatre perhaps ten times in his life. He was auditioned by Dullin, allowed to attend classes at the Atelier school free of charge, and on 8 September 1931, his twenty-first birthday, appeared on stage for the first time, as a servant in *Volpone*.

'An influence is an encounter', Barrault wrote.

> One cannot be influenced by anything one does not already embody. Better than an encounter, it's a recognition. It is the accelerated revelation of our own personality thanks to another person's experience.
>
> (1972, p. 62)

Barrault's first important meeting was with Dullin; Barrault recognised that Dullin's

> genius lay in the fact that he remained essentially and constantly an authentic human being, and that he could create around him[self] an atmosphere of apostleship and absolute artistic purity and integrity.
>
> (1951, p. 13)

The quality Barrault recognised in Dullin is one we have seen in Copeau and Decroux and is one we shall see later in other modernists who espouse a doctrine of artistic purity that has a profound moral dimension as well as an artistic one. Perhaps Barrault's desire to direct a troupe was born from admiration of Dullin's moral and artistic strength.

'Everything is a sign. Who called? Was it me, or the Atelier? Was I wrong to call it my *second* birth, and Dullin a *second* father?' (Barrault, 1972, p. 67). Barrault's discovery of his vocation was a homecoming. At the Atelier, Barrault studied improvisation with Dullin, working on authenticity of sensations and feeling before expressing. They improvised, as Copeau had with his students, on the themes of birth, discovery of self and the environment, the emotions, animal behaviour, animal characteristics in people and human characteristics in animals, in addition to studying the classics and gymnastics. The example of the Ecole du Vieux Colombier was still very much before the eyes of Dullin and the others who had been touched by Copeau's seminal ideas. In Sokoloff's Stanislavsky class, Barrault studied, for example, a box of matches, then had to describe it from memory. He then became a match, as if it were a person. Dullin introduced his students to Meyerhold's ideas as well as Stanislavsky's, and Barrault especially liked Meyerhold's 'We cannot enter the world of the theatre except through the world of sports.' Or, as Artaud would write later, 'The actor is an athlete of the heart' (1958, p. 133).

If Barrault's meeting with Dullin was an accelerated revelation of one aspect of his personality, his meeting with Decroux uncovered another aspect of that same rich and complex self. Barrault remembers that he and Decroux researched objective mime and subjective mime. Objective mime, useful in creating illusions, was based on the premise that the 'imagined existence of an object will become real only when the muscular disturbance imposed by this object is suitably conveyed by the body of the mimer' (Barrault, 1951, pp. 27–8). Barrault calls this study of counterweights the key to objective mime. The study of objective mime had a clear link to the silent pantomime of the nineteenth century in that it involved the creation of illusions such as walking in place, walking against the wind, climbing and descending stairs, and other depictions of actions and objects in the external world. Whereas nineteenth-century pantomime was, as far as we can tell from the surviving visual and written records, primarily an affair of the extremities – the more easily moved face, hands, and arms – Decroux and Barrault's work was more physical, and illusions were created with the whole body, especially the trunk; hence the name 'corporeal mime'.

Subjective mime Barrault defines as the 'study of states of the soul translated into bodily expression. The metaphysical attitude of man in space.' (Barrault, 1951, p. 28) Whereas objective mime had existed in the nineteenth century and was simply treated in a different way in the twentieth, subjective mime is a purely modernist invention, and probably did not exist in the nineteenth century, just as modern dance, also concerned in its way with 'states of the soul translated into bodily expression' did not exist before Isadora, Ruth St Denis and Ted Shawn. This study of subjective mime was an

> intoxicating study which lifts you up to the level of religious art. When we were pursuing our researches [sic] into subjective mime we felt we were drawing near to Oriental actors; we felt we were discovering all over again the plastic art of Greek tragedy.
>
> (Barrault, 1951, p. 28)

If objective mime found its expression in illusions, subjective mime was expressed in Decroux's research in the areas of *statuaire mobile* (mobile statuary), *homme de songe* (men in a state of beatific reflection) and *méditation*, areas that have been called abstract by some, but which for Decroux were always firmly rooted in the concrete, no matter how abstract they might seem to the inexperienced viewer. Decroux was able to translate the study of counterweights from objective into subjective mime, and often in his lessons spoke about how an actor carrying a heavy physical weight closely resembled one carrying a heavy metaphysical one. Again we find mention of religious art, the oriental actor and Greek tragedy linked to Decroux's research. Decroux's goal in this work with Barrault, like Copeau's goal before him, was to return to the sacred source of drama. It was as far from commercial entertainment as it could be, and in fact would have failed had it simply entertained. The struggle to return to this sacred source was modern (and classical as the two often resemble each other) in its rigour, in its purity and in its singleness of purpose.

Whereas in Copeau and Decroux one sensed an almost ascetic doctrine, in Barrault's writing and work one sees more easily the intuitive man, the dreamer and the *bête de théâtre*. One cannot imagine a Copeau or a Decroux spending the night on stage at the Atelier as Barrault did, asleep in Volpone's bed, and later describing it as having 'spent my first night of love at the source of my art' (1972, p. 77). Not first of all an intellectual or analytical personality, Barrault possessed a lively imagination that found an echo in the American transcendentalists, quotations from whom filled his notebooks during his Atelier period.

Barrault's love of American literature led him to William Faulkner's *As I Lay Dying*, a novel whose theatrical possibilities he began to explore during his last year at the Atelier. The visionary quality of the novel struck him deeply, acted as a catalyst and served as a 'totem around which I could collect all the ideas and sensations that I had accumulated on the theatre' (Barrault, 1972, p. 84). He was attracted to the non-verbal behaviour of Faulkner's primitive characters. While Barrault's goal was to work in

64

a way that was as different from pantomime as it was from the way he had worked with Decroux, he had no preconceived theory or dogma. He wanted instead to discover the more intuitive, animal aspect of mime. In Barrault's adaptation of Faulkner's story of a mother's illness, her desire to see her coffin made before her eyes by one of her children, and her eventual death, Barrault found not pantomime but the silent moments of speaking theatre. He later described it as mostly 'a question of speaking actors who didn't say anything' (Weiss, p. 4). This was the distinction Decroux and Barrault made between the mute nineteenth-century pantomime, silent originally because of governmental restriction, and the new twentieth-century mime's ability to choose silence, or vocal mime, or speech.

'In *As I Lay Dying* a certain wild young man tames a horse even wilder than himself', explained Barrault, who as a young man often called himself a *fauve* (wild beast). 'Now this horse appealed to me from the miming point of view. So it was from the point of view of the horse that I worked at *A I Lay Dying*' (1951, pp. 30–1). Vocal mime as well as spoken text played an important part in Barrault's adaptation of the Faulkner novel under the title *Autour d'une mère*. Vocal mime, which began in the improvisations at the Vieux Colombier, continued in Decroux's teaching and performance, quite naturally found an important place in Barrault's first performance piece, and later figured importantly in Jean and Marie-Hélène Dasté's *Sumida* (Jean Dasté's performed in *Autour d'une mère*).

The only noise I allowed myself [in *Autour d'une mère*] was the rhythm trodden on the boards by my bare feet, the wizard beating of my heart, and a whole poetry of breathing.

It was theatre in its primitive state.

For text: merely two brief explanatory scenes in cut-and-dry prose, and this was anyway a concession. And two long lyrical monologues said by the mother after she was dead. The songs: two choirs of several voices without a valid text and for the most part murmured; in tune, thanks to a tuning-fork whose discreet note came to us from the wings.   (Barrault, 1951, p. 36)

Barrault's exploration of vocal mime, which he called a 'whole poetry of breathing', in one scene of *Autour d'une mère* translated the mother's death agony by

a long series of calculated breathings that made a ghastly effect, corresponding with the scrapings of the saw of the carpenter-son, who on his mother's instructions, was, during her agony, making her coffin.

(1951, p. 39)

Was *Autour d'une mère* to Barrault what *Les Demoiselles d'Avignon* was to Picasso? In the quotations cited above, Barrault uses the word 'primitive' in describing first the characters in Faulkner's novel, then his theatrical treatment of them, which he also describes as a 'totem'. He describes his mime style as 'purely animal' and his character as a 'wild young man'. Barrault was more Dionysian and intuitive than his master Decroux, who was often Apollonian and cerebral in his modernism. In them we see the two primary tendencies of modernism – which might colloquially be termed the 'messy' and the 'neat'. The messy branch includes Van Gogh and Jackson Pollock; among the neats are Mondrian and Brancusi. But Barrault distinguished himself from his teacher, as all students must if they are to become artists, by exploring the intuitive side of his nature in opposition to Decroux's more analytical perspective.

Yet both tendencies were certainly present in *Autour d'une mère*, which Artaud describes as a 'great, young love, a youthful vigor, a spontaneous and lively effervescence' flowing 'through the disciplined movements and stylized mathematical gestures like the twittering of birds through colonnades of trees in a magically arranged forest' (1958, p. 145).

Artaud's evocative description of Barrault's performance reinforces the emphasis on the primitive in Barrault's own writing about *Autour d'une mère*. Artaud's essay is studded with words such as 'magic', 'sacred', 'incantation' and 'witch doctors':

> But his [Barrault's] work uses the means of the theatre –
> for theatre, which opens up a physical field, requires
> that this field be filled, that its space be furnished with
> gestures, that this space live magically in itself, release
> within itself an aviary of sounds, and discover there new
> relations between sound, gesture, and voice – and
> therefore we can say that what J.-L. Barrault has done
> is theatre.   (1958, p. 146)

The kind of magical, incantational theatre Artaud is describing here, accompanied by an 'aviary of sounds' produced through body percussion and vocal sounds, found new relationships between 'sound, gesture, and voice'. It was evidently far removed from the white-faced, silent pantomime of the nineteenth century; it had been given back its voice and its vitality through contact with Asian and African theatre forms, which seemed to Barrault and other modern artists to be more vital than the prevailing, enervated European forms.

Jean Dorcy describes a solo performance Barrault did some years later entitled *Maladie–agonie–mort*, based on the death scene of *Autour d'une mère* (it figured in the 1945 programme outlined in the previous chapter):

> Suddenly the bust draws itself up, the right arm desperately extended toward the sky; – A second of absolute immobility; – The extended arm is lowered, palm turned toward the ground, slowly, very, very slowly; – the arm passes before the head, before the neck, before the bust, thus blotting out life . . .   (1961, p. 56)

This was no doubt the kind of performance Artaud had in mind when he wrote that, in order

> to reforge the chain, the chain of rhythm in which the spectator used to see his own reality in the spectacle, the spectator must be allowed to identify himself in the spectacle, breath by breath and beat by beat.
>
> (1958, p. 240)

In *Autour d'une mère* Barrault had accomplished, albeit sooner than Decroux had expected it to happen, what Decroux had prescribed in *Words on Mime* as his cure for a sick theatre. This two-hour-long drama contained a half-hour of spoken text; the characters spoke only to themselves. The mother spoke after she had died, for, as Barrault wrote, 'Words only appear on the far side of reality' (1972, pp. 86–7). The 'alien arts' were practised by the actors themselves, vocal mime was used, and the text, if not written by the actors, was at least chosen and arranged by them. It appeared that the revolution in acting that Decroux had recommended had taken a surprisingly short time to complete itself. (In fact, this one victory would soon be almost erased in theatre history by a counter-revolutionary trend, the tremendously popular film *Les Enfants du paradis*, to be discussed later.) The initially hostile audience at the first performance of *Autour d'une mère* was won over, and gave Barrault and his colleagues an ovation. The theatre emptied, and only Artaud was left, drunk with enthusiasm.

'After the strong personality of Charles Dullin', Barrault wrote, 'and the exacting (yes, as exacting as Alceste) friendship of Etienne Decroux, I have been most impressed by the grandiose character of Antonin Artaud' (1951, p. 48).

> What did [Artaud] awaken in me? With him, it was the metaphysics of theatre that entered through my pores. Until then, thanks to the training at the Atelier, the night spent in Volpone's bed, and those two years spent with Decroux, I was introduced to the physics of the human body. . . . Oriental approaches that I discovered through my readings, suggested by Artaud, made me suspect horizons other than the very clear one of the flesh. (1972, p. 105)

Barrault's work soon led him into films; after *Numance* and *La Faim* (experimental, modern-mime productions that used vocal mime and text and which followed on from *Autour d'une mère*), Barrault produced work with more well-developed texts that allowed less room for movement, vocal mime and mask work, and so for the tradition stemming from Copeau in the Ecole du Vieux Colombier. One could say that Barrault chose instead to continue the line of the *theatre* of the Vieux Colombier, which, despite the genius of its director and many of its actors, was a commercial enterprise, and as such depended upon box-office sales for its continuation, and hence was subjected to the kinds of compromises all commercial theatres are forced to make to stay afloat. After *Autour d'une mère*, *Numance* and *La Faim*, Barrault would never again be able to say, with quite so much authority, that the play 'didn't exist as a text. It is only a group of actors and a director working on a stage. It's theatre trying to purify itself . . .' (1972, p. 84).

Decroux thought Barrault could have been one of the two or three best mimes in the world, but chose instead to be one of the two or three hundred best speaking actors in the world. In conversation with me, Madame Dasté argued that to be a great mime

is not really what he chose. He chose to assemble a company and together with it to bring to life the plays he loved best, or sometimes those [plays] he hoped would help him to survive for a while, to be his own Maecenas, and then return to what he really loved and believed in.

Madame Dasté alludes to the problem so well described by André Gide in his evaluation of why Copeau's theatre failed:

He [Copeau] was struggling against the epoch as any good artist must do. But dramatic art has this frightful disadvantage, that it must appeal to the public, count with and on the public. This is indeed what made me turn away from it, more and more convinced that truth is not on the side of the greatest number.

(Gide, 1948, p. 139)

Jean Dorcy's evaluation of Barrault is similar to Decroux's. Dorcy laments that Barrault has 'left the house of mimes', and imagines that Barrault's great success as a primarily speaking actor and director 'does not gratify him'; like Decroux, Dorcy suspects that Barrault is not 'struggling against the epoch', or, at least, not struggling enough. Dorcy addresses Barrault directly, suggesting that Barrault's work must mean nothing to him and that 'the future awaits a new kind of interpreter, who will not need a director. The setting is mere window-dressing. Today, the emphasis must be placed on muscle. You know it Barrault' (1961, p. 113).

In 1979 Barrault wrote that forty years of trying to use his body as an instrument in the theatre had transformed him as a religious conversion might have. For the body he had 'contracted a religious fervour' (1979, p. 71). In the years following 1946, however, that religious fervour was expressed primarily in films and plays in which movement served in great measure as support for or illustration of a dramatic text, rather than, as it had in *Autour d'une mère*, *Numance* and *La Faim*, as a primary element. Never again would the stage be as bare, the bodies be as nude, the risk be so great. Barrault has said that, when he left Dullin and the Atelier and moved from Montmartre to Saint-Germain-des-Prés, 'leaving the ivory tower of an aesthetic golden age, I pushed with lowered head into the society of humans' (1972, p. 92).

Of the post-Atelier period, Barrault admits that perhaps Decroux was somewhat correct in his evaluation of Barrault's character: 'I spread myself thin. Instead of persevering in the underground caverns of theatrical research, I responded to all of life's temptations' (ibid., p. 111).

For the next two decades of Barrault's career, his work alternated between acting in films and producing, directing and acting in theatre, using the money he earned in the first to subsidise his work in the second. This busy schedule left little time for experimentation along the lines he had begun to explore with *Autour d'une mère*.

In 1943 Jacques Prévert, at Barrault's suggestion, wrote the scenario for a three-hour film based on the life of the famous nineteenth-century pantomime, Jean-Gaspard Deburau. Deburau was silent in his performances because of government regulations limiting the number and *genre* of Paris theatres; French theatre and film during the German occupation were similarly censored, and Deburau's story was an ironically appropriate one to tell at that moment in history. Marcel Carné directed the film during 1943–4, amid shortages of electricity, costume materials, wood and plaster for sets, and even motion-picture film, and in unheated studios. The film was entitled *Les Enfants du paradis*, the name given to the poor who could afford only the cheapest theatre seats far up in the balconies of the theatres which lined the Boulevard du Temple, called the 'Boulevard du Crime' in the time of Louis-Philippe because of the offences enacted daily on its stages. The scenario of *Les Enfants du paradis* presents the life of a beautiful woman, Garance, played by the legendary film actress Arletty. Garance inspires three kinds of love in three different men: love from the head, love from the heart and from the flesh (echoes of François Delsarte's trinity are heard here; Delsarte was the late-nineteenth-century singing-teacher who innovated a way of looking at the expressive potential of the human body long before body language was a catchword). She chooses a fourth, for love of money.

Garance's three suitors are historical figures in Paris of the 1840s: Deburau (played by Jean-Louis Barrault); Frédérick Lemaître, a famous melodrama actor of the period (played by Pierre Brasseur); and the killer known to all Paris at that time, Pierre-François Lacenaire (played by Marcel Herrand). Anselme Deburau, Jean-Gaspard's father, was played by Etienne Decroux.

The film was a great critical as well as popular success; while it is often shown as one of the most important French films ever made, its significance in this study is the role that it played in the development of twentieth-century mime. The film appeared at a time when the new modernist tendencies in mime had taken root. Decroux's role as master teacher and discoverer of modern mime was well established, but his antipathy to performance made him almost invisible. It was clear that, if modern mime was to appear outside Decroux's atelier, it would have to be brought above ground by a student of brilliance. Barrault was such a student, and his first performances as a mime in a recognisably 'modernist' vein had been a great critical if not popular success; as Barrault wrote years later, 'there were so few people who really understood it [modern mime]. Hardly anyone appreciated it then' (1951, p. 29). Barrault went on to a more successful career as a film actor and a producer, director and stage actor. One can only conjecture what would have happened had Barrault not gone into the speaking theatre, or if *Les Enfants du paradis*, with its seductive images of nostalgic and charming nineteenth-century pantomime, had not been made.

After Barrault, another student of great promise did not appear until Marceau came to Paris after the Second World War. *Les Enfants du paradis*, made during the war, was first shown in 1945. The pantomime sequences depicted were created with the help of Georges Wague, the last in the line of Pierrots who traced their lineage directly back to Deburau. The pantomime sequences in the film, although based on nineteenth-century scenarios, and true in spirit to the performances of the time, certainly reflect some of the research Decroux and Barrault had undertaken on objective mime, while completely ignoring the research in subjective mime, which of course would have been inappropriate in a historical re-creation. In 1946 Barrault did a stage version of the pantomimes he performed in *Les Enfants du paradis* entitled *Baptiste*, reinforcing in the public's mind the nineteenth-century image already well established by the film. In 1946 Barrault made a film entitled *Baptiste*, based on the stage perform-ance of the same name.

'I admit to having been a bit unfocused in my desire to learn everything about the human body,' Barrault confessed, 'whereas Decroux didn't want to lose his focus and closed himself in. There you have the two mistakes. This is where we parted company. He wanted to become pure, absolutely pure. As for me, I wanted to love everything' (Dobbels, 1980, p. 54).

Barrault has had a long and varied career as a stage and film actor, and founder and director of a theatre troupe which has been a landmark on the Parisian landscape for decades, as well as touring frequently outside France. He has produced a large number of new plays over the years, and has also been a prolific and lively writer on the theatre and on his own work. One can understand a Decroux's or a Dorcy's disappointment that Barrault didn't continue in mime, but Barrault, after mastering his body, became a speaking actor by choice rather than by default. This chapter does not follow Barrault into his later work after, as Dorcy says, he 'left the house of mimes'. Some might argue that he never did – the house of mimes is perhaps just larger than anyone thought.

4
Marcel Marceau

I am a prisoner of my art. People do not want to see
me speak, or use props or appear as a character other
than Bip or the stylized mime that I have created.
They are uneasy with a Marceau that is unfamiliar.

(Marcel Marceau)

Copeau's original premise, one of his intuitive leaps in
actor-training, was to cover the face of the student actor
so that his body would be forced into greater expressivity.
From this central idea, the importance of the core of the
actor rather than his extremities, modern mime was born.
This is the major difference between modern mime and
the nineteenth-century paradigm it sought to replace; in
the work of Jean-Gaspard Deburau and his successors,
the face and the hands were of primary focus, working
overtime to make up for the verbal language that had
been forbidden.

How, then, can we explain Marcel Marceau? He is the

most visible mime of our time, yet he seems not at all to come from the modern roots we have examined. He performs alone, without speech or vocal mime; his face is painted white and his basic body stance, pelvis tilted slightly back as if sitting down, face and hands thrust correspondingly forward toward the audience, places more emphasis on the extremities than on the core. If we have found modern mime and modernism in the other arts to be saturated with oriental and African influences, Marceau seems to owe more of a debt to the European tradition of *commedia dell'arte* and the American silent film than to any wrenching-away from Western traditions. If most of modernism seems to have disdained the bourgeois and challenged its basic assumptions with anarchist–socialist–surrealist images and manifestos, Marceau has been clutched to the bosom of the international cultural elite. His work, rather than challenging the political, social or artistic *status quo*, seems instead to ratify it by keeping silent in a world which is screaming with social injustice and impending ecological disaster. The sketches he performs so brilliantly are less controversial in the twentieth century than Deburau''s performances were in the nineteenth. Deburau had silence imposed upon him; as an outcast from the mainstream theatre of Paris, he wordlessly commented upon the foibles of the authorities and injustice of his situation. Marceau, by contrast, has chosen silence and uses it to depict charming stories about dating-services and people walking dogs and selling balloons. He has briefly and unsuccessfully tried to take off that mask; it has, however, stuck fast, and, like the victim in his sketch *The Maskmaker*, he is trapped inside an image he might otherwise wish to have outgrown.

Marceau's career can be divided roughly into four periods. The first (1939–47) is his artistic gestation, culminating in his first public performance as Bip in 1947 at the Théâtre de la Poche in Paris. From 1947 to 1952, Marceau's work was two-pronged; while he continued developing and performing Bip sketches and pantomimes of styles,[1] he worked with a company of several actors presenting large-scale mimodramas. The programmes that Marceau performed during this period were made up of solo works as well as company works in which Marceau figured as the leading actor and the director. In 1952 Marceau started frequent international touring, and Bip rather than the company did most of it. From then until 1964, when the company was officially laid to rest, company work and solo work were separated, and considerably more solo than company performances were given. Since 1964 Marceau has performed in the largest auditoriums the world over, as many as 300 times a year.

Marcel Marceau is the most difficult of the Big Four (Decroux, Barrault, Marceau, Lecoq) to write about. The ephemeral nature of his work (mostly performing, less teaching or writing than the other three) lends itself less well to critical analysis, and a straightforward narrative of his life does little to suggest his importance. His career has been long enough for him to have come in and gone out of fashion with certain critics; some of the theatre-going public to whom he introduced mime now find his work *passé* while new audiences are just discovering him. The current global interest in mime would certainly not exist were it not for Marceau's thirty-odd years of international touring, and the high public visibility

---

[1] Marceau's solo programmes have always been divided into two parts: Pantomimes of Style and Bip. In theory, the earlier sketches demonstrate techniques without characterisation whereas the latter are mini-dramas. In practice, there is little difference.

he has had for most of that time. One might say that he has been as visible as Decroux has been invisible.

This high visibility has had the disadvantages of its advantages, as the French say. Marceau has broken ground and blazed trails, and now his name is synonymous with mime. But most people agree that mime needs to be bigger than one performer, and every mime performer in the last thirty years has, in one way or another, been in Marceau's shadow; but even his teacher Decroux and his mentor Barrault have profited from Marceau's success. Decroux first taught and performed in the United States as a result of the interest stirred by Marceau, and Marceau has focused the world's attention on French mime and theatre in an arresting way that has no doubt benefited Barrault. When Marceau first performed outside France in 1947 on tours of Switzerland, Italy, Belgium and Holland, the artistry and novelty of his work, its brilliance and its direct appeal, were immediately recognised and appreciated. The public and the press adored him everywhere he went. In a world recovering from the ravages of a cataclysmic war, the presence of a lone figure in white face sporting a top hat with red flower must have given some laughs to audiences who were tired of crying, tired of trying to figure out a world gone mad. Pain and disappointment with the present can foster nostalgic backward glances to seemingly happier and simpler times.

Decroux responded to his young student's success by quickly moving past the illusionistic techniques he had developed during Marceau's apprenticeship with him. There can be little question that Marceau's commercial success led Decroux to explore more esoteric areas of mime, as Decroux found it important to eliminate easily exploitable aspects from his teaching after he began to be identified as Marcel Marceau's teacher rather than for anything that he himself had done. As Marceau's audiences grew larger and his popularity increased, Decroux grew even more rabid in his art-for-art's-sake approach, more of a holy zealot who might still accuse art, as he first had as a student at Copeau's school, of being a publicity-seeker while politics was a saint.

Since Marceau has seemed to represent mime for so long, attempts by other performers to grow past his image into a more contemporary one seem sometimes, inaccurately, to be a repudiation of the man himself. Marceau and mime have been synonymous for decades; as a result some mimes have attempted to free themselves from what they have felt to be the public's overwhelming expectation that all mimes should be in his image. Marceau himself must often have wanted to leave behind the image he so successfully popularised, or at least stretch it a little. When he has ventured too far from Bip, as he has in several films over the years, his work has met with a less than warm reception. The post-war European public he first distracted from the bleakness of their everyday lives was replaced by a world public of upper-middle-class theatre-goers, a kind of well-fed, well-dressed silent major-ity who are happy with his approach, but for reasons different from the ones that first made him a success. All aspects of the image Marceau has made famous have been questioned by other mime performers, who have, by using the word 'mime' or 'pantomime' to describe their work, immediately set up an expectation that they would be like Marceau: a charming Pierrot or Baptiste or Bip in white face who creates illusions and images through movements of face, hands, and body, but who does not speak. In essence, a silent storyteller.

This absence of words places the burden of the story-telling on the performer's movements, and these movements will, then, out of necessity, be mostly objective mime, illusionary techniques and counterweights which carry the meaning of the performance. As a result, the area of subjective mime, that part of mime that translates the internal movements of thought and spirit (sometimes considered to be 'abstract'), is more or less absent from most objective-mime performances. It is in the area of subjective mime, the area of moral and spiritual counterweights, that mime is most truly modern (André Malraux observed that nineteenth-century arts tell a story and twentieth-century arts do not); yet most audiences continue to expect the mime performer to be an objective, silent storyteller, and not a modern artist who with vocal mime and perhaps some text (as in *Autour d'une mère*) attempts to follow the movements of thought and spirit. Modern dancers, too, attempt to depict the journeys of the soul, in contradistinction to the nineteenth-century ballet's mimed stories with interludes of dancing. Yet the mime's movement vocabulary and centre of gravity are different from those of either a ballet dancer or a modern dancer.

Like all good modernists, Decroux rebelled decisively against the nineteenth-century paradigm, which he first became acquainted with as a child. He recalls in *Words on Mime* that when he first saw a Pierrot communicate without words, he was displeased, and found the speaking actor less of a blabbermouth. On the same subject Decroux later said,

If I've been impressed by all the arts, even if not equally impressed by all of them, there is one that frankly displeased me. And that is pantomime. Pantomime: that play of face and hands which seemed to try to explain things but lacked the needed words. I detested this form. But that's rather strange because pantomime was always supposed to amuse people.

(Mime 1978, see bibliography)

As Marceau began his career, he had before him the example of his teacher, Decroux, destined to spend the rest of his long career in the catacombs of research and development. And he had the example of Barrault, who had begun in the *avant-garde* world of *Autour d'une mère* and moved into the world of films and plays, always keeping his great flair and skill for movement. The aspect of Barrault's mime which had met with immediate and unqualified popular success was the *Baptiste* pantomime which he performed after his success in the film *Les Enfants du paradis*. Barrault said he might still be performing pantomime plays had he found authors capable of providing scenarios for him (how this echoes Copeau's predicament!); or perhaps he felt too restricted by the limitations imposed by this historical *genre*.

If Marceau did not want to follow Decroux into the catacombs of his craft, neither did he want, nor did his abilities fit him, to follow Barrault into the speaking theatre. Marceau could not become Baptiste, since Barrault was still playing that role from time to time in the late 1940s, so he became Bip instead. It is perhaps only natural that a sensitive young actor, following the difficulties of the war years in France, would look back to a romantic past rather than forward to an uncertain future in a modern art that was having trouble defining itself and for which there was virtually no audience and almost no critical support. Marceau chose to go back behind the gauze curtain that the actor Plancher-Valcour broke though in 1789, shouting 'Long live liberty!' There are no simple answers to why he found this inevitable, or why audiences have responded so profoundly and affirmatively to his choice.

Marceau saw strength in the hybrid performed by Barrault in *Les Enfants du paradis* and made a brilliant career from it, incorporating even more of the strong physical underpinnings he discovered in his study with Decroux, adding to that basis the astute observations he made of Chaplin and Keaton, combining them with the white make-up, the charming costume and the storytelling vignettes which through the particular often communicate the universal. If his training was in modern mime, there is still the essence of nineteenth-century romanticism in Marceau's work. Copeau, in collaboration with Jouvet, had done away with footlights and invented spotlights, which could easily light an upright figure almost anywhere on the stage. This innovation changed acting-style more than we might suspect. It is natural that modern mime performers and modern actors are more upright, more bipedal, than their nineteenth-century counterparts. The upright actor of theatre's golden ages performed outdoors in natural light coming from the sides and from above; Copeau wanted to return to those golden ages, and he did it by going forward, with innovations in theatrical lighting as well as in acting-technique. In fact, Marceau performs as if he were in a ninetenth-century theatre, his face painted white like that of his predecessors, hands and face usually aimed outward as if toward the footlights, from which they would once have caught the weak light originating from gas jets or reflected candles. This peculiar starting-position was described by Jean Dorcy thus: 'Drooping shoulders, slightly rounded back, knees bent a little, such is the initial silhouette from which Bip . . . will arise' (1961, p. 64).

One could argue that Marceau's work falls well outside

the modernist aesthetic: brief stories silent except for musical accompaniment (which was also used in the nineteenth century) and with apparent beginning, middle, and end (characteristics of much of Marceau's work) are clearly creations inspired by an earlier, less fragmented and less sophisticated time. Eyes accustomed to the disassociations and sudden juxtapositions of cubism, or the confrontational nature of *Ubu Roi*, might find Marceau's vignettes mostly pretty and charming, two adjectives that cannot usually be applied to modern art, which rediscovered the 'primitive', the subconscious and irrational, the importance of the broken surface, the ragged edge, the bold, dripping, seemingly unfinished line, the surreal. Even when Marceau deals with war and social injustice, the form is usually tastefully composed, balanced, refined and even tidy. Marceau's performance looks quite at home in the culture palaces of the world. The classical music which accompanies many of the sketches is easy on the ear, and has none of the dissonances and surprises associated with modern music.

'The actor-mime *vibrates* like the strings of a harp. He is *lyrical: his gesture seems to be invested with a poetic halo*' (Dorcy, 1961, p. 104). So Marceau describes his work. The lyricism, the poetic halo, seem to be remnants of a romantic era, not important elements in a modern one. Marceau's pantomime seems more romantic and nineteeth-century than it is a reaction against that paradigm, in the costume and make-up, the basic body stance, its muteness, and the anecdotal charm of the vignettes.

The name 'Bip' is derived from Pip, a character in Charles Dickens' *Great Expectations*, a novel Marceau read as a child. As a child, too, he saw Chaplin's film *The Circus*. 'To us, he [Chaplin] was a god. As a boy I sat entranced in motion picture houses, watching those shining images unfold before me. It was then that I determined to become a pantomimist' (Marceau, 1958, p. 59). (Here we might remember that Chaplin, too, was silent from necessity and not from choice.) The seven-year-old Marceau was already performing for local children, and at his aunt's summer day camp, dressed in his father's trousers, wearing a painted-ink moustache. From Strasbourg, where Marceau was born, his family first moved to Lille, and later Limoges when the Second World War broke out. There Marceau's father, killed in 1944 at Auschwitz, was a kosher butcher – Marceau remembers watching admiringly as his father carried whole quarters of beef. In Limoges, where Marceau and his brother Alain worked for the Resistance, Marceau changed ages on identity cards with red wax crayon and drawing-ink to make men seem too young to be sent to labour camps. Marceau also led hundreds of children disguised as boy scouts across the Alps to safety in Switzerland.

Marcel Mangel became Marcel Marceau when he moved to Paris in 1944 with a false identity card provided by his brother. In Paris he took a job teaching theatre in a children's school in Sèvres, where Eliane Guyon, then a student of Etienne Decroux's, was also a teacher. Marceau enrolled in Dullin's school, where he met Decroux. Marceau, like Barrault before him, played a small part as a servant in *Volpone*; and, like Barrault, he studied one-on-one with Decroux.

In 1946 Marceau joined Barrault's company to perform in the *Baptiste* pantomime Barrault created after the success of *Les Enfants du paradis*. In 1947, Bip was born. Decroux had first introduced Marceau to the role of Harlequin, and as he did his research he wondered why such a character couldn't become part of the twentieth century. That year Marceau played Bip on one side of

Paris, Harlequin in Barrault's *Baptiste* on the other side, and continued daily studies with Decroux. Marceau's work with Decroux eventually came to an end as performance took precedence over study.

Marceau's brilliant career as a solo artist has completely overshadowed, in the public's mind, the twelve years during which he spent some of his time and most of his income from solo performing working with his troupe, with whom he wrote and directed more than twenty-five mimodramas. In one early piece, entitled *Le Tribunal*, vocal onomatopoeia, tone and articulation played as important a part as body movement and facial expression. Newspaper reviews of later pieces do not mention the actors' use of voice, but do indicate that almost all the works performed by Marceau's troupe harked back to the eighteenth or nineteenth century for inspiration if not actual scenario; that all the mimodramas were concerned with storytelling (Gogol's *The Overcoat*, for example, was rendered in mime), which suggests that the movements performed by the company were illustrative and anecdotal; and that, while usually quite popular with audiences, these mimodramas seemed to some critics as too often involving stereotypical characterisations in clichéd situations.

In 1955, after years of successful European touring, Marceau performed for two weeks at the Phoenix Theatre in New York. His spectacularly successful engagement there was extended, and then he transferred to the Ethel Barrymore Theatre, and finally to City Center, for a total of six months of continuous performances. Marceau's television performances at this time opened up mass audiences; Marceau had become a household word, and defined his art for millions who never knew it existed before seeing him on the Red Skelton television special.

His performances in New York were followed by a tour of the United States and Canada.

His tremendous popular success was paralleled by a resounding critical success. Most critics have been moved and thrilled by the virtuosity of Marceau's performing. Eric Bentley, writing in the *New Republic* of 10 October 1955, found that in *Youth Maturity, Old Age, and Death* 'the lyrical is raised to the power of the sublime' and ended by calling Marceau's performance an 'evening of great, of quintessential theatre'.

There has been a small group of dissenting critics who have said of Marceau's work that 'What it lacks utterly is a mastering *necessity*' (Hayes, 1960, p. 46). In a similar vein, Harold Clurman found Marceau's pantomimes 'illustrations of cute observations, enjoyable for their graceful *bonhommie*, but without any substantial creative meaning' (1955, p. 370). Richard Gilman in 1983 felt that Marceau 'too often . . . stretches things beyond their intrinsic worth or offers us either what we already know or what we have no compelling interest in knowing'.

Marceau's imitators, and they are legion, have copied the highly successful synthesis Marceau has made; what they have not bothered to do, for the most part, is to learn the basics of corporeal mime, the study of which (along with his innate, quite wonderful abilities) enabled Marceau to accomplish what he has. They are working with pre-digested materials. These aspiring pantomime artists have copied the make-up and the costume, the choreography and the facial expressions; they miss the core, the body, the foundation and perhaps the talent. While it is true that many dancers perform *Swan Lake*, most of them with much the same choreography, such dancers have spent ten or twelve years in the classroom, where they have acquired a wide range of movement skills which enable them to perform *Swan Lake* one day, *Rodeo* the next or a Balanchine ballet the next. In dance, the equivalent of the typical imitator of Marceau is a performer who specialises in reconstructions of period dances from a certain epoch, and is incapable of dancing anything else. Like period dance, period mime has a certain quite specific style, a specific placement of hands, head, arms, and evokes a specific time and place.

Meanwhile, Marceau is a giant, albeit a somewhat controversial one. His supporters counter criticism by asserting that it is motivated by professional jealousy of one of the most phenomenal solo performers of our century. Some supporters, however, have been heard to express dissatisfaction that Marceau's work has grown so little in forty years. One might be tempted to reply that when you start at such a high level there is little distance left to go, but no doubt talent of Marceau's quality raises high expectation.

Marcel Marceau is a master of a period art known as silent pantomime. He is one of the greatest pantomime artists the world has known; but his work has as little to do with modern or post-modern mime as nineteenth-century ballet has to do with modern or post-modern dance.

5
Jacques Lecoq and Mummenschanz

There is not just one form of mime. Mime is everything. First of all, mime is theatre.

(Jacques Lecoq)

If Marceau has made his career primarily on stage, synthesising and popularising work derived from Decroux's and Barrault's research, metamorphosed by his own sense of theatre and his own uncanny ability to understand his audience, Jacques Lecoq has spent most of his career in the classroom. He began teaching physical education at the age of nineteen, and teaching has been his real vocation ever since. At first he 'taught theatre people to move' in the way he had taught 'athletes to swim' (from an unpublished interview with Lecoq by Frances McLean).

In 1945 he began to work with Jean Dasté's Comédiens

de Grenoble, where Lecoq's fencing-abilities perhaps more than his acting-skills got him the job of chor-eographer and actor. Copeau's son-in-law, Jean Dasté was imbued with the spirit of the Ecole du Vieux Col-ombier, having participated in that fertile experiment, and it was in Grenoble, in the morning classes under Dasté's direction, that Lecoq first learned to wear a mask.

'The mask demands', Dasté has written, 'both simplifi-cation of gesture and amplification; something pushes us to the extreme limit of the feeling to be expressed. If you are supple, if you have studied acrobatics or dance, the gesture has a dimension that is much larger' (1977, p. 89). We hear echoed in these words the ideas of Copeau and his disciple Michel Saint-Denis and almost everyone who has been touched with the spirit of the Ecole du Vieux Colombier: simplify and amplify.

Little by little, having understood the major ideas of Copeau through Jean Dasté and Léon Chancerel, Lecoq became a teacher of mime and theatre, and after two years in Grenoble he returned to Paris, where he taught for a year. In 1948, at the start of his eight-year residence in Italy, Lecoq founded the Teatro del'Università di Padova and began mask work with Amleto Sartori, the now-renowned maker of leather *commedia* masks. In 1952 Lecoq founded the School of the Piccolo Teatro in Milan, with Paolo Grassi and Georgio Strehler. From 1954 until 1956 he was director–choreographer for sixty productions in Syracuse (Greek tragedy), in Rome (at the Opera), in Venice (for the music of Luciano Berio, for whom he choreographed *Allez-Hop* and *Mime, Music Number Two*) and at the Piccolo Teatro (productions with Dario Fo and premieres of plays by Ionesco).

Lecoq's eight years in Italy taught him

the sense of having my feet firmly planted on the ground, something which we maybe didn't have in France at that time, where there was a lot of dreaming going on, or where themes came from the imagination. There was [in France] a sort of surrealism in the air.

(McLean interview)

In Italy Lecoq discovered Ruzzante, *commedia dell'arte*, and later, in Syracuse, tragedy. Like Copeau before him, Lecoq found the two poles that have since influenced his teaching: Greek tragedy and Italian *commedia*. Both types of theatre were performed outdoors, used large body gestures and were collaborative ventures. Both used masks, and as a teacher Lecoq has from the beginning worked with neutral (at first called 'noble') masks as well as with expressive ones. The mask is the central tool in Lecoq's teaching.

Since his return from Italy to Paris thirty years ago, he has operated one of the most successful and influential theatre schools in the world. Lecoq has been one of the great teachers in late-twentieth-century mime, yet he is not a mime, has never studied mime, and does not like mime. Like Copeau and Decroux before him, he is an outsider destined to revolutionise an area in which he was not at first a specialist. The mime he has taught is a mime 'open to the theatre much more than a mime for solo performers, or a mime which would be completely silent. I made mimes speak' (McLean interview). Lecoq again quite deliberately included mention of words in a description of his teaching he wrote for the twentieth anniversary of his school in 1976: 'Trees, fire, water, wind, and earth explode into characters, into letters, names and words.' *Pantomime blanche* is taught at Lecoq's school as a period style, one of the many approaches to theatrical performance, and not as the one approach to performance, as it is in Marceau's school.

In 1962 Lecoq added to his already well-developed and well-known research in neutral mask a branch of exploration Copeau had opened with the Fratellini, clowns:

> Before that, nobody spoke about clowns in the theatre; that remained . . . in the circus, and then we started working on clowns and the clown in relation to himself; to the search for one's own clown . . . a clown of the theatre. (McLean interview)

The clown, too, wears a mask, albeit a small one – a red nose. After exploring clowns, and adding the richness of this area of research to his expertise as a teacher, Lecoq undertook a study of melodrama, the larval mask, half-masks and the *buffon*.

According to Lawrence Wylie, a Harvard professor who spent a sabbatical year with him, Lecoq is an 'intuitive being in the tradition of Bergson and Bachelard, but his method, unlike theirs, is fundamentally Cartesian' (1973, p. 22). According to Lecoq himself, 'Every time I have had an experience, it fed the teaching-process, and basically it all developed like a plant growing' (McLean interview). These stimuli have continued throughout Lecoq's teaching-career; among them is his experience (since 1969) of teaching architecture students at the Ecole des Beaux Arts in Paris.

With the architects, Lecoq 'discovered space, light, colour; all these things I've brought back to the school. The school has a store of experiences gathered from different spheres and furnished by random chance' (McLean interview). The work with the architects has resulted in the development of the Laboratoire d'Etude du Mouvement as part of Lecoq's school. An undated flyer for the Laboratoire lists the following areas of study as part of its programme: sensitising of the body to space; analysis of movement; the dynamism of forms and colours; an organic approach to words; sound transfers; the drama of constructed spaces; playing of passions, states and situations; gauge of the body; dynamic objects; spatial structures of the body; portable architecture; animation; masquodrome; video; projects.

What Lecoq calls 'random chance' is perhaps the intuitive aspect Wylie mentions; the Cartesian aspect, the interest in and desire to analyse movement, dates from Lecoq's early days teaching sports. While protesting that he has never studied mime, Lecoq admits that certain ideas were in the air in France following the Second World War. Certainly the ideas of François Delsarte, late-nineteenth-century French singing-teacher, were part of the cultural baggage Lecoq as well as Decroux inherited. The Delsarte trinity (head, heart, pelvis) figures prominently in Lecoq's writing as well as in his brilliant mask lecture–demonstration, *Tout bouge* ('Everything moves'). Delsarte's identification of intellectual, spiritual–emotional and physical centres in the body is at the basis of Lecoq's work.

'Tragedy and *commedia*', Lecoq has said, echoing Copeau, 'were for me two stages in a theatre, a total theatre in a way, but a theatre of maximum scope where the actor was extended to his limit. That began to be very important – without trying to make a museum out of it.' Lecoq's work with Jean Dasté was preparation for his Italian period, where Lecoq made discoveries that, coming after his work with mask and improvisation, were to form

92

the basis of his teaching. When Lecoq returned to Paris, his

> school started with one student, Elie Pressmann, who
> is now a dramatist, and who came and said, 'Where is
> Lecoq's school?' I said, 'It's here.' He asked, 'Are there
> any other students?' I said, 'No, you are the first.' And
> then I gave a lesson. He put on his tights and I gave
> him a lesson in movement.   (McLean interview)

It was not by accident that Lecoq began with a lesson in
movement, and today his letterhead reads 'Ecole Jacques
Lecoq, Mime, Mouvement, Théâtre'. Also on the letterhead a line-drawing in red of a masked Harlequin
figures prominently. Lecoq considers Harlequin a 'key
personage to what goes on in the school. He has a tragic
element on the one hand and a comic element on the
other. He really unites the two poles of what I love in the
theatre' (McLean interview).

Over the years the increase in the school roll has made
it necessary to hire other instructors, but all of them have
studied at least two years at the school themselves, and
many have completed the third year Lecoq offers for
students who plan to be teachers. As a rule these teachers
have stayed with Lecoq ten to twelve years.

> The spinal column of the school is the analysis of
> movement. Analysis of movement is not necessarily the
> analysis of the body, it is the analysis of all movements,
> even of animals, of plants, of the dynamics of passion,
> of colours, of everything that moves. We are trying to
> get to the bottom of movement.   (McLean interview)

Getting to the bottom of movement reveals that, 'when

an arm is raised, it creates in us a corresponding dramatic state, and that an attitude of the body is related to an internal attitude of mind' (Rolfe, 1978, p. 152).

This analysis is carried out by Lecoq and by his students.

> There is an exchange which takes place between the students and me. . . . the students often have wishes . . . which are often the right ones. They aspire to theatrical forms which do not exist as yet and I find it interesting to do things which haven't yet been done. But, of course, the theatre which hasn't been done yet is reflected in the past. It isn't possible to say that one is always inventing new things, there are points of reference, so that permits me to recognise periods in the past which are propitious. But it's not a museum, it's an exchange which takes place in the present. Nevertheless, tradition interests me, but by that I mean a tradition which is rediscovered through the phenomena of today, rather than trying to redo something which has been done already. . . . One imagines the past, and the thing that I find good is that the past helps us to imagine the future. (McLean interview)

The voice of Jacques Copeau is heard more than a little in these words.

Lecoq describes his teaching-method thus: 'Instead of talking about the moon to a child, we both go and look at it.' This looking at the moon is not always a totally pacific experience, as

> by dint of teaching one knows that the crises are necessary, and, even when once a class didn't undergo a crisis, I created one artificially. . . . they [the students]

felt themselves too at home, too mollycoddled. They were having this calm and tranquil life and I said to myself, 'If they don't have a crisis, what's going to become of them?' (McLean interview)

One student quoted by Lawrence Wylie described her work with Lecoq in this way: 'Jacques Lecoq strips you completely and gives you your true identity; for the first months I was on the verge of tears . . . you go through a long process of discovery during which he reveals you to yourself.' Wylie cautions the reader that these revelations are never psychological in nature, but are based entirely on the work at hand, the 'implications of movements, of objects, of human reactions' (Wylie, 1973, p. 27). Another student found that Lecoq's 'school is like sandpapering yourself all over. When you're all sanded down, you hurt, but you feel more' (Levy, 1978, p. 62).

Like the Ecole du Vieux Colombier before it, the Ecole Jacques Lecoq teaches by analysis and by improvisation. The classes which deal with analysis break down gestures and activities into teachable sequences, activities such as cutting wood, throwing a disc, mixing a complicated cocktail in 181 steps, or climbing a wall in fifty-three steps. In these steps we are reminded of photographs of Muybridge or the diagrams of Hébert. Analysis is the first stage. The second is reassembling the elements, changing and modifying different aspects in order to change and modify the meaning of the sequence. Classes which deal with improvisation lead toward synthesis, toward identification with forces, objects or beings. For example, the student is asked to improvise the life-cycle of an oak, from acorn to full-grown tree. Other themes for improvisation include the four elements in their various manifestations; substances such as glass, rubber, steel, milk and oil;

colours, sounds, plants, animals and finally human beings. Like students at the Vieux Colombier, Lecoq's students are encouraged to develop powers of observation which fuel these improvisations.

> An artist's talent and art consist in finding in three lines the essence of whatever he is painting. At our school we try to recognise elements in life which take place before acting them out, a recognition of live things through the body, through mimism. In this manner we get to know trees, the rhythm of the sea, colours, space of people, all that is alive and moves which is infinite.
>
> (Unattributed interview with Lecoq)

Although exercises in any school change from year to year, it may be useful here to describe some improvisation exercises at Lecoq's school during the late seventies. One example is 'The Absent Host'. Ten or twelve students are asked to imagine that they have been invited to a large party. Lecoq describes the setting, where the furniture is placed, where the food is placed, and so on. As the title of the exercise implies, the host is absent, and as the guests arrive one by one they are required to react spontaneously and naturally to the setting and each other. The point of the improvisation, which continues for perhaps five minutes, is to tear away learned theatricality, to get rid of caricature, to pare away acting which is unneccessary and false.

Another example is 'The Swimming Pool'. The goal of this group improvisation is to react intelligently to the space of an imaginary swimming pool, and the people in it. As the space of the pool (the edges, the water, deep water, shallow water) varies, and as the people vary (some you know, some you don't; some you would like to know, some you wouldn't), so the student's reaction must vary accordingly. A variation on this exercise has cops chasing robbers through the pool.

'The Bar' is a solo improvisation in which the student is required to imagine sitting in a bar when a second, imagined person enters, looking for his hat. The student's reactions must change appropriately as he or she realises that he or she is in fact sitting on the hat. (Details from Jim Calder, unpublished interview.)

Improvisations with neutral masks, made for Lecoq by Sartori in Padua, draw attention away from the face and focus it on the body. The individual wearing the mask becomes one 'without past, without knowledge, without preconceptions, and ready to discover a new world'. As Lecoq once described the neutral mask,

> the minute you put on a mask that covers your whole head, you are transformed. Your own person ceases in that instant and you are what happens. We all communicate with our faces, mouths, eyes, the way we hold our heads, the lines that are etched into our skins. With the mask, you have no past, no race – except what the mask portrays. . . . It forces you to act with your body, to think with your body – and the body doesn't lie. (Levy, 1978, p. 50)

Lecoq's improvisations then shift from explorations of elements to explorations of humans who have personalities dominated by certain elemental or animal characteristics. These improvisations use expressive character masks, also made by Sartori. The characters depicted by these masks are ones easily found in Padua – timid, sly, miser, Jesuit: *commedia* characters all (ibid., p. 51). Afterward, students work on dehumanised improvisations with larval masks

(masks with unformed or faintly formed features), large unpainted Basel carnival masks, grotesque masks, half masks (which permit speech), and finally the smallest mask, the red nose. The challenge in these exercises is to embody in form, speed, intention, rhythm and so on the shape and quality of the mask.

Deliberately to portray with the body a message opposite from that of the mask is a technique known as 'counter-mask'. (In more traditional acting-techniques, playing the opposite characteristics to the dominant ones of a character gives depth and is known as 'playing the opposite'.) Lecoq is at his best as an actor when he demonstrates the countermask, placing the face of an imbecile on the well-articulated and beautifully held body of a sophisticate. Masks

> allow one to search for the pivotal point within an action, within a conflict; allow one to find the essential, the gesture that will epitomize the many gestures of daily life, the words of all words. All that is great tends toward immobility [immobility is also a gesture].
>
> (Rolfe, 1978, p. 153)

At the end of their third semester, students spend three weeks carefully observing an activity in Paris which was before totally unknown to them. Students have, for example, worked in hospitals, funeral homes, religious communities, schools for the deaf, and so on. At the end of this period of research, each student performs for his fellow students and the school faculty what he or she has learned from that period of observation. *Autocours* is a word Lecoq uses to describe the work students do on their own, working together to prepare scenes that will be presented in class. One such class had as its assignment the depiction of one day in the life of a village, from sunrise to sundown. Thirty-five students created all aspects of village life, including all the diverse characters one finds in a small town anywhere. In a smaller *autocours*, four to eight students were asked to present through movement the essence or spirit of an artist or author. The exercise of portraying village life is one that fosters skills of observation and depiction, whereas the artist/author exercise engages the imaginative powers in an exercise in transposition.

In the second year students study *commedia dell'arte*, *pantomime blanche*, Greek chorus and its relation to the hero, and the experience considered by all to be the most difficult and the most rewarding in the Lecoq method, the search for 'one's own clown'. One's 'clown' is inextricably related to one's essential weakness, which one must 'recognize, bring out, hold up, publicly make fun of, and incidentally, make people laugh' (Wylie, 1973, p. 27). While clowns 'are people who try to do everything well and fail', *buffons*, another rich area of exploration in the Lecoq syllabus, are 'deformed creatures that make fun of life' (Levy, 1978, p. 57).

The Lecoq school has since 1956 trained an impressive number of theatre professionals. Among the better known in France, listed in a 1981 newspaper article about the twenty-fifth anniversary of the school, are Pierre Byland, Philippe Gaulier, Claude Evard, Philippe Avron, Bernard Douby, Alberto Vidal, Ariane Mnouchkine, Liliane de Mermadec, Pierre Richard and Pierre Debauche (*Libération*, 4 December 1981). As the greater number of Lecoq's students are not French, the international register of Lecoq's prominent students would be a good deal longer; and, indeed, most of the world's leading teachers and performers of mime have been taught by either

Decroux or Lecoq. Among the most well-known of Lecoq's students outside France are the members of the Swiss mime–mask troupe Mummenschanz, to be discussed below.

Jacques Lecoq has an intuitive understanding of some essential elements of theatre; and, owing to his genius as a teacher, he has communicated these principles, treasured earlier by Jacques Copeau, to several generations of students from all corners of the globe. Lecoq's teaching is responsible in large measure for the renaissance of interest in *commedia dell'arte*, the neutral and expressive mask, and the clown as a theatrical type not confined to the circus. Lecoq's teaching has been a perfect antidote to Decroux's; if either one had not existed, he would have to have been created, probably by the other. Decroux is a pure modernist, a wonderful anachronism in the eclectic post-modern world. His teaching is based on a sense of the moral worth of art. Lecoq is already something of a post-modernist in that he foresaw the synthesis that was to come and has in fact encouraged it. He assumes a more flexibile, less austere, more pragmatic approach than Decroux. His teaching is perhaps more outward-looking, whereas one senses that Decroux looks inward for his sense of direction. Lecoq came from a background of sports and kinesiology, in which he was trained to analyse movement; went into theatre training ('the border between sports and theatre was not well defined' – McLean interview), which certainly had some vestiges of Hébertism in it; encountered Paul Bellugue, and through him, or from the spirit of the times, picked up elements of the research of François Delsarte and Paul Souriau.

Although Lecoq never studied with Decroux, the fact that they have been the two major (sometimes considered rival) mime teachers in Paris for three or four decades means that they influenced each other, even if that influence could be seen to have led them in diametrically opposed directions. Lecoq once said he found Decroux's approach 'too negative, too cubist, and too abstract. It might have been good for Decroux himself and his disciples, but I recognized that it would never evolve, never allow the student to develop his own personality, his own art' (Levy, 1978, p. 49). Although Lecoq's assessment of Decroux's work may have been accurate for a certain period, the rich crop of artists now performing who studied with Decroux from the mid-1960s through to the early 1980s certainly have developed their own personalities and their own art. As the seminal teachings of Jacques Copeau are at the source of both Decroux's and Lecoq's work, each teacher having branched off in a different direction from the same trunk, there are more similarities than differences in their basic ideas. The differences come from differences in personality, teaching-techniques, taste, world-view and generation. The similarities are striking: emphasis on the expressive potential of the body and the correspondingly secondary importance of text, decor, costumes and other elements; the importance of ensemble work and improvisation.

When Lecoq says that he taught mime to talk, he is well ahead of most performers or audiences. 'There are schools such as ours', Lecoq has said, 'which can be in advance [of the times] and foresee a little the theatre which may be coming' (McLean interview). Lecoq's school is one of those theatres that, rather than being a résumé of what has happened, has helped young performers find new directions and so revitalise the theatre. Lecoq's whole vision of the theatre is like Copeau's, and his students, like Copeau's, remain on the fringes of the commercial theatre, not wanting to give themselves to it as it exists.

They, like their teacher, work apart, preserve their artistic vision, nurture their strength, and steadily increase their power to influence the course of theatre history.

The most visible representatives of Lecoq's teaching, the Mummenschanz company, two Swiss mime and mask performers and one Italian (Andres Bossard, Bernie Schurch and Floriana Frassetto), made their first European tour in 1973 and in the autumn of that year appeared for the first time in the United States. On 30 March 1977, after having made four American tours and at least as many in Europe, Mummenschanz opened at the Bijou Theatre on Broadway in New York. They were virtually ignored by the press, but managed to hang on for three months, during which they were enthusiastically reviewed by Clive Barnes of the *New York Times*. An avalanche of good press followed, and the little 350-seat theatre, which before had been rather sparsely attended, began to sell out. But in December of that year Mummenschanz were obliged to perform in Paris at the Théâtre de la Ville. In order to be in two places at once, the original troupe created a second Mummenschanz troupe, which took over the Broadway theatre in October. This and successive replacement troupes continued on Broadway through eight performances a week for three years, something which has not happened to a mime company before or since. (Marceau performed for six months on Broadway in 1955.) In 1978, while two Mummenschanz troupes alternated on Broadway, another company, performing in identical costumes to identical choreography, toured the United States. Meanwhile, the original company toured European festivals. For one year there were four Mummenschanz troupes performing simultaneously. It didn't take this European troupe long to discover the American practice of franchising. Of the Broadway replacement troupe one reviewer said,

> One could complain that the comic timing is not as sharp as it might be, that some of the more subtle aspects of the pieces have been passed over for quick and easy laughs, that a costume here and a mask there are beginning to look a little frayed and much repaired. But that is not the issue. There is mime on Broadway. And that mime is not of the classical, storytelling variety. It is a curious blend of masks and body-disguising costumes, anthropomorphic creatures, human abstractions, and symbolic confrontations. It is clever, funny, occasionally thoughtful and witty, entertaining, and a commercial success. (Cocuzza, 1979, p. 4)

The Broadway run finished in 1980. In the United States the original Mummenschanz company became, like Marceau before them, media celebrities, appearing on many network television shows. In 1980 the three took a much needed sabbatical year, and met again in 1981 to begin work on a new performance. In 1984 a new Mummenschanz play was born, and the cycle of performing and touring began again.

Mummenschanz's first programme, which they toured for six years, was composed of many masked solo, duet and trio compositions in which the reality of the human body was often distorted or altered in some way which was provocative and disorienting for the audience. For example, the front of the body became the back, or the top became the bottom, the costume providing a head between the legs and concealing the real head by a tail. Another device concealed the body completely and did away with head, arms, dorsal and ventral sides of the body, reducing it to what appeared to be a blob of primeval slime, or a beanbag. When the human body was evident, it was clothed in a black unitard and wore a cubistic structure over the head. This head-covering could be altered for dramatic effect by the wearer or by another performer. One especially striking mask had rolls of toilet paper in place of facial features, the unrolling of the paper indicating talking; in another, one performer wrote on the paper tablet of another's face, and, in yet another, one performer's mask (composed of uncooked pizza dough) was sculpted by another. In another memorable mask, modular units (cubes) from one mask were placed into corresponding holes in another. Audiences responded audibly to these abstracted yet truthful depictions of the ways individuals communicate with one another. In an interview in *Mime Journal* (no. 2) in 1974, Andres Bossard described how the Mummenschanz arrived at these abstractions.

at first it's a very naturalistic work. Then it's cut cut cut till we have the initial pattern coming through. While we are discussing the improvising, we think to make it accessible to the audience by purifying it of all our anecdotal stuff. Then it's a drama which is *our* drama but everybody can fulfill it with his own life, put himself in it.

The second programme, which the company began to perform around 1984, had larger masks which extended well beyond the performer's body and filled large parts of the stage. To construct these masks/costumes/scenic elements, the performers–creators used the newest, lightest and strongest materials created by modern technology. Bossard, Frassetto and Schurch worked for three years in their large workshop in Zurich exploring the theatrical possibilities of styrofoam, foam rubber and paper-thin yet super-strong plastic membranes. Their second programme incorporated these newer materials while developing further some of the elements used in the first (the giant 'slinky' toy, for example). The human figure was less visible in the second programme as their performance became more abstracted, yet audiences continued to respond to something they could recognise, some basic humanity they could successfully project onto these shapes. The second show, like the first, was an ingenious exploration of the dynamic qualities necessary to make abstract shapes comprehensible to a general audience.

The abstract shapes and sounds of the futurists, the dadists, the surrealists and the Bauhaus theatre would be hooted off almost any commercial stage in the world today. Some reconstructions of Oscar Schlemmer's Bauhaus ballets have been presented for initiates at places such as the Museum of Modern Art in New York, but they could never play in the kinds of theatres to the kinds of audiences Mummenschanz attracts. The Joffrey Ballet has re-created the surrealist ballet *Relâche* (a collaboration of Satie, Picabia and Rolf de Mare), but the audiences that regularly cheer the Joffrey do it for the other ballets. The Mummenschanz synthesis, which has much in common with object animation, puppetry and black-light theatre as well as mime and mask work, owes as much to Jacques Lecoq as to Craig's essay on the super-marionette. It is as if, suddenly, fifty years of rather difficult material, research that had a dangerous edge, had been rendered respectable, amusing and even appropriate for children. The *Chicago Sun* said it nicely when it suggested that Mummenschanz had been formed by a *committee* composed of Jacques Tati, Paul Klee, Marcel Marceau, Toto the Clown, Tristan

Tzara and Lewis Carroll, with the assistance of Charlie Chaplin, Buckminster Fuller, Harpo Marx and René Magritte. Most audiences recognise and respond to anecdotal dynamism beneath the abstracted forms, and, probably much contrary to the intention of the performers, spend as much time trying to figure out how many bodies are in the form and *how* on earth are they doing that as the audiences at pantomime performances spend trying to figure out *what* the performer is doing. In either case, audiences feel rewarded when they succeed.

The second Mummenschanz performance was specifically designed for large theatres, culture palaces the world over. Marceau's image is barely visible from the last row of these theatres, but the gigantic inflated bags and twenty-foot-high masks read easily from that distance and greater. As they continue to tour widely, so Mummenschanz continue to impress on the public consciousness that mime can be something other than Marcel Marceau. Moreover, just as Marceau opened up performance possibilities for other white-faced pantomime artists, so Mummenschanz have inspired similar groups, using similar techniques and raw material.

Their mentor Jacques Lecoq, whose life is research and development, not presentation and performance, has said, '[success] can be dangerous. They have had too much success; they don't know what to do with it. . . . One must be very strong to start all over again, to say "It's working, let's stop . . ."' (Buhrer, 1984, p. 40). Mummenschanz is important because, for the first time, a general audience is being exposed to modern mime in the way that it has been exposed to, say, modern painting, modern dance or modern architecture. It is not the spare, difficult and sometimes academic modern mime of Etienne

Decroux, but it is not the charming, white-faced, anecdotal work of Marceau either. It may be pop-modern mime, but it *is* modern.

6
Post-Modern Mime

Webster's Dictionary, helpful as always, defines
'modernism' as 'the philosophy and practices of
modern art; *esp.* a self-conscious break with the past
and a search for new forms of expression'. A requisite
of modernism was a disenchantment with past
masters. . . . The good postmodernist, on the other
hand, enjoys a respectful educated acquaintanceship
with the moderns; indeed, he often makes his living
by teaching them to students. . . . He can go nimbly
through the motions that cost the moderns some
agony. Instead of cleaning out the attic, he lives in
one, among the dusty friendly busts of Proust and
Joyce, Kafka and Rilke and Pound.   (John Updike)

Updike's definitions of modernism and post-modernism
(albeit in literature rather than in mime) help us to see
why Marceau is not a modernist; why Mummenschanz is
on the borderline between high-modern and post-modern;

and why the post-modern mimes (new mimes) and new vaudevillians revel in synthesis and hyphenated arts.

Marceau has not sufficiently rejected the past to be modern; instead of self-consciously breaking with the nineteenth-century paradigm as other modern artists did, he rather embraced the spirit of nineteenth-century panto-mime. It is evident that he did not detest the older paradigm with the same ardour as Decroux and Lecoq did, or rebel against it with as much energy. Mummen-schanz goes 'nimbly through the motions that cost the moderns some agony'. Yet they are not fully post-modern in that they have not incorporated elements typical of post-modernism: a political dimension, an irreverence, a self-consciousness or self-referential theatricality.

Post-modern mime is an outgrowth of modern mime in the same way as post-modern dance, painting, theatre, architecture and music are extensions of the modernist phases of their arts. The modern phase of these arts has been better known that the modernist phase of mime, best represented by the rigorous, almost religious purity of the work produced by Etienne Decroux, which for fifty years has been all but invisible, an underground art for an initiated few. There are perhaps only 500 or 1000 people anywhere in the world who have seen that kind of modern mime and who can identify it. Because of Decroux's aversion to performing and because of the inherently transitory nature of performance, repeated viewings were impossible. Whereas modern painting became the pre-vailing paradigm in much the same way as modern architec-ture did, the prevailing paradigm for mime in the second half of the twentieth century was not the modernist phase of that art, which was hidden away in Decroux's basement, but instead the form made popular to audiences around the world by Marcel Marceau, who hybridised some modern mime techniques with what is basically a nineteenth-century romantic form of silent storytelling, delightfully witty in content, tastefully crafted in form, closer to the nineteenth century than to the twentieth, closer to Deburau than to Decroux.

Certain of the modernists in every art have produced work that is spare, cool, classical, abstract and modular. Modernist architecture, product of the Bauhaus, presents a much discussed and written-about example. Buildings in this style have been popular enough to transform many cities into labyrinths of glass-sheathed steel structures that resemble rectangles of graph paper cut out and pasted on to the skyline. They are abstract, pure machines for living and working, which through central heating and air-conditioning are cut off from their environments; and, were it not for the view from the window on the twenty-eighth floor (when it is not of more modern buildings), inside such a structure one could be anywhere in the world. The engineering-discoveries of the late nineteenth and early twentieth centuries meshed auspiciously with the prevailing aesthetic of the times, and what was the most practical and cost-efficient (at least in the short term) became what was artistically popular as well.

Post-modernism in architecture is easily definable because modernism in architecture was the established way of building; there was a certain univalence in architecture that has not existed in all other modern arts. The post-modern building is more eclectic, less pure, less single-minded. The post-modern building is variegated in its integration of often conflicting styles and even humour. It is asymmetrical, personal, perhaps whimsical, colourful, paradoxical. It is often more ecologically sensitive, relying less on central heating and air-conditioning. Critics of the style may call it arbitrary. One of the distinguishing characteristics of post-modernism in architecture is that it revels in showing what used to be hidden, like the backstage in Trisha Brown's *Set and Reset*, a typically postmodern dance with decor by Robert Rauschenberg which reveals rather than conceals the once-secret backstage. The architectural equivalent of this is the Centre Pompidou in Paris: a modern building turned inside out becomes a post-modern one. It is still made of glass and steel, still modular, still sleek and polished, but with every pipe, conduit, duct, vent, brace and rivet exposed. Just as Trisha Brown is not stage centre in her compositions in the way nineteenth-century ballerinas were, supported by the *corps* (or at the emotional centre of the drama the way Martha Graham was), so the Centre Pompidou does not have a central entrance behind which one finds a large lobby and grand staircases.

Modern painting also achieved widespread acceptance, so that the approved list of contemporary painters and sculptors is represented in modern museums the world over. Every museum in the world has to have its Willem de Kooning, Alexander Calder, Henry Moore, George Segal, Francis Bacon, Jasper Johns, Roy Lichtenstein, and so on, in the same way as every American city has to have a Howard Johnson and many have their own Calder industrial orange stabile situated in the heart of the office district. Just as the styles of these artists are perhaps more various than the styles within modern architecture, so the post-modern equivalents in painting are more various. Not all modern painting was as pure and essential as Mondrian's work. Certain painters were fascinated with the irrational, the dream state, the subconscious, the primitive, and some post-modernist painting (the neo-expressionists) can be seen to be more closely allied with

111

them rather than with the more mechanical or hard-edged moderns.

Architecture and painting have been big business for some time. Even though modern painting didn't start out that way, it has become a multi-million-dollar industry in New York City alone. The primary function of modern art was, Suzi Gablik wrote, to

> create a critical consciousness; but more often than not, this critical function has simply disappeared, as mass bureaucratic culture assimilates potentially subversive forms of art and deprives them of their antagonistic force by converting them into commodities.
>
> (1984, p. 52)

The lesson of this age, she continues soberly, is 'that art cannot survive along the capitalist "faultline" except by being compromised' (ibid., p. 54).

Still, even in their most subverted forms, painting and sculpture have been able to remain highly individualistic, as they can be viewed by a large audience over a long period of time. They can also be acquired by an individual owner. And modern buildings, even if not at first appreciated by the people who use them, soon blend into the landscape and are taken for granted (with some notable exceptions) as they function as buildings. The Eiffel Tower, which raised an extraordinary ruckus when it was built, became the symbol of Paris; now more visitors visit the Centre Pompidou, which raised a similar wave of protest, than climb the Eiffel Tower.

Live performances, however, cannot be viewed over a long period of time; for their successful presentation (not necessarily commercially successful), they demand the presence of a certain number of people in the same room at the same time as the performance, and they cannot be acquired by an individual collector, hung on a wall or used as offices or dwellings. Theatre has always been behind the other arts in innovation for this reason, and the words 'popular' and 'subsidised' must always accompany 'theatre'; without a large audience in which everyone pays a little money (popular art) or a small audience that pays a lot of money (patronage) there is no professional performance. For this reason most innovation has come from amateurs who have subsidised their own work and performed for a small band of initiates. Copeau noticed that his work could not exist along what Gablik calls the capitalist faultline without being compromised; Decroux advises his students to earn their living outside the arts; Lecoq rails against the dangers of success.

Compared to modernist experiments in theatre, modern dance and modern mime have an even more difficult time, to which the fact that they are almost unknown to anyone except the few practitioners of these esoteric arts contributes. To realise their vision, modern-mime and modern-dance choreographers have had to train students to perform a distinctive style. The early modern dancers in America and modern mimes in France were visionary artists, working in basements or lofts or other spaces no longer suitable for commercial activity, hence available at low rent to artists, and performing for small audiences of initiates; these artists worked at the physical, economic and social margins. Modern dance was never big business in the way modern art and modern architecture have been, but it did get to the point of becoming business – some observers say, to its detriment – around 1960. The second generation of modern-dance companies which came into being in the 1950s and 1960s 'survived, if they survived at all', says Marcia Siegel, by figuring out how to look more acceptable to their audiences, their critics, and their backers. In one sense, modern dance now [1973] is just going through what happened to most of the other arts long ago. It is establishing a popular version of itself.   (1977, p. 153)

Not all post-modern choreographers felt this need for popularity; Merce Cunningham continues his post-modern choreography with as little regard for popular appeal as his modernist forebears. Modern mime established a popular version of itself with the Mummenschanz company and similar companies which were able to synthesise the analysis of the previous fifty years and present it in a way that was palatable to popular audiences.

Perhaps theatre passes alternately through periods of synthesis and periods of analysis. Copeau certainly had a vision of a *whole* theatre, but the methods he employed to attain it, the research he provoked, led to more than fifty years of analysis of movement, mask work, circus skills, voice and other skills which are just now beginning to be reintegrated into a whole again. The post-modern period is a period of synthesis, but it is not simply a return to the ideas of Copeau; despite his vision and foresight, he allowed his effort to come to an end (at least, Gide speculated that he did) because the authors he hoped would appear to provide scripts for a new theatre did not. Contemporary performers, fuelled by half a century of research, are now following the advice of one of their mentors, Etienne Decroux. They have done away with the author as an individual separate from theatrical activity. The author, if there is one, is increasingly the actor himself. The odd division of labour that had the author sitting down, thinking and writing, and the actor standing up, performing as his mouthpiece, is as schizophrenic an

114

arrangement as is imaginable, reminding one of other equally absurd yet seemingly unnoticed divisions we take for granted in our time.

Post-modernism at its worst is an eclectic hodge-podge, a popularisation of hard-won discoveries, a co-opting of the pure vision of modernism. At its best, post-modernism is a vision of completeness, an integration of disparate elements into a resonant whole, a synergetic work that heals as it takes audience and actor simultaneously backward to their common roots and forward to their shared destiny. Post-modernism in its finest examples reintegrates the mind, voice and body in a return to the ancient period when the poet spoke, sang and mimed his own poem. (There was no play-acting, no 'method' required, although complex techniques and skills were used then as they are today.) The performance of ancient as well as of the modern mime comes from the heart, manifests itself first in movement and then continues into speech; unhindered by political considerations, it is normal for one who has a voice to speak. Pure modern art is transformed by global consciousness in the information age into post-modernism. The artist feels compelled to speak out on the burning issues of the day, using whatever techniques communicate most effectively. Peter Schumann writes in his 'Why Cheap Art? Manifesto',

People have been thinking too long that art is a privilege of the museums and the rich. Art is not business! It does not belong to banks and fancy investors. Art is food. You can't eat it but it feeds you. Art has to be cheap and available to everybody. It needs to be everywhere because it is the inside of the world.

(Fago, 1985, p. 16)

115

The post-modern information glut has put the world at our doorstep.

> All art is faced with starving children and apocalyptic politics. All art is ashamed and angry and desolate because of its impotence in the face of reality. To inject bread baking into art production seemed like a healthy thing to do. (Ibid.)

Schumann is speaking here of his transformation from a 'normal frustrated city artist' into the founder and director of the Vermont-based Bread and Puppet Theatre, where every August for the last ten years he and others have presented the Domestic Resurrection Circus. The Bread and Puppet Theatre is a post-modernist theatre ensemble which uses an eclectic array of techniques (puppetry, theatre, dance, storytelling) to treat complex subjects which are themselves about synthesis and juxtaposition of seemingly disparate topics (in 1985, Nicaragua and Bach; St Francis and nuclear holocaust were subjects in a previous year).

One of the earliest manifestations of post-modern mime occurred when pure, analytical, mostly silent mime, imported directly from Paris, home of modernism, by R. G. Davis, crashed headlong into the political, artistic and social ferment of San Francisco, described then by *Time* magazine as the Athens of the counterculture. Davis moved to San Francisco in 1958, where he and his students gave their first performances in 1959. In 1960 the *Eleventh Hour Mime Show* was presented weekly at the Actors Workshop, then one of the most progressive theatres in America, and in 1961, after presenting Beckett's *Act Without Words II* (a pure, analytical modernist work; Beckett, the good modernist that he is, has some plays

116

27. Dulcinia Langfelder in 'Vicious Circle'. Photograph Paul Martens, ©
Winnipeg International Mime Festival.

28. Leonard Pitt in 'Not for Real'. Photograph © Philip Kaake.

29. French mimes Claire Heggen and Yves Marc. Photograph © Delahay.

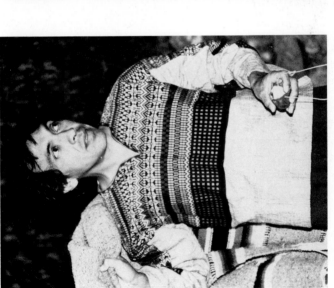

30. (*left*) Mexican performer, teacher and festival impresario Sigfrido Aguilar. Unattributed photograph.

31. (*right*) F.J. Bogner, West German psycho-clown. Photograph © W. Flögel.

32. Post-modern storyteller and performance artist Jim Calder. Photograph © Plauto.

33. Three Czech mimes. From left to right: Boleslav Polívka, Boris Hybner, Ctibor Turba. Photograph © RTE, Dublin.

34. Denise Boulanger and Jean Asselin in a duet created for them by Etienne Decroux. Photograph © Daniel Collins.

35. Jan Munroe and Ian Cousineau in Munroe's 'Wood Would, Wouldn't It?'. Photograph © Elissa Zimmerman.

36. New Vaudevillian Bob Berky. Unattributed photograph.

37. Ronlin Foreman, an American post-modern clown who studied with Lecoq. Unattributed photograph.

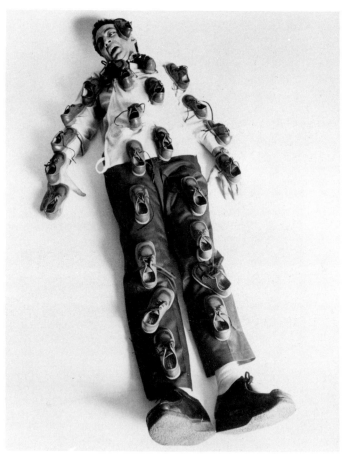

38. Paul Zaloom, plastic puppeteer and performance artist. Photograph © Jim Moore, 1986.

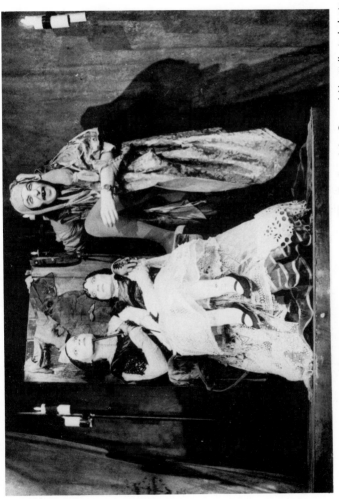

39. Boleslav Polívka, Czech mime-clown and Chantal Poullain in 'The Fool and the Queen'. Unattributed photograph.

40. Friends Mime Theatre in a parade in 1979. Photograph © Kathy Kohl.

41. (*left*) Denise Boulanger and Rodrigue Proteau in 'Alice'. Photograph © David Peterle.

42. (*right*) Denise Boulanger and Francine Alepin in 'La Dame dans l'auto'. Photograph © Line Charlebois.

43. (*left*) Argentinian post-modern mime Benito Gutmacher. Photograph © Gapihan.

45. Tony Brown and Kari Margolis in 'Deco-Dance'. Unattributed
    photograph.

46. Belgian mime troupe Pyramide op de Punt. Photograph © Alain Chagnon.

47. 'Backlight' performed by Grifteater, 1983. Photograph © Maarten Brinkgreve.

48. New Vaudevillian, clown and eccentric dancer Bill Irwin. Photograph
© F.B. Stimson.

49. New Vaudevillian and clown Geoff Hoyle. Photograph © F.B. Stimson.

composed only of words and some plays composed only of movement), Davis and company began their first experiments using words with mime techniques (Toscan and Ripley, 1975, p. 22). While there were other mime groups in the United States at that time and earlier (Paul Curtis founded the American Mime Theatre in 1952), most of them continued in analytic modernism rather than beginning post-modern synthesis.

This is one of the first re-entry points of mime back into the theatre, at least in the United States, and one of the most significant in terms of a lasting influence. Some of Copeau's students separated mime from theatre, and except for a few brief, tentative attempts it had remained separate, developing on its own as a pure modernist (or even regressive nineteenth-century) form. The re-entry did not happen just once, but continued to happen many times, as artist after artist experienced the collision between mime practice and the post-modern, informational age and was driven to construct his or her own theatrical synthesis.

These early experiments in San Francisco resulted in a performance of *The Dowry*, a *commedia* play adapted from Molière's *Scapin* and Goldoni's *The Servant of Two Masters*. The production, performed with masks on a raised portable platform, must have looked much like the ones Copeau directed. Copeau had begun his experiments with *commedia*; *commedia* is the door through which mime left the theatre, and the door through which it returned.

It was not until 1965, after having produced Brecht's *Exception and the Rule*, that the troupe began to realise the political potential of theatre, and began to study Marxism. From that time on, all the emerging political and social concerns of that particularly tempestuous time, and in that particularly charged atmosphere, literally found voice (remember Valcour tearing open the scrim and shouting, 'Long live liberty!') in the work of the San Francisco Mime Troupe. High art had come home to the people. The playwright was no longer separate, and, from that time on, plays were made by the troupe, or freely adapted from other sources by the troupe. The playwright for whom Copeau had been waiting finally appeared on the scene, the playwright Decroux has predicted would arrive, the playwright to whom the theatre belongs: the actor. The San Francisco Mime Troupe actor–mimes are first and foremost members of a larger political, social and economic community, not modernist loners living in a garret, on the fringes of society, producing pure art. The San Francisco Mime Troupe, a threatre which spoke directly to the common man, performed then, as it does now, in a park. As Stanley Kaufmann observed in *New Republic* on 16 December 1978, 'Everything flows, everything has been worked out communally by the group, and everything is borne on an assumption of community with the audience.' Of course that sounds easy, but in practice is difficult to achieve. 'Socialist art', Suzi Gablik writes,

> deprives us, on the whole, of formal and aesthetic qualities, being strong on message but often weak art; whereas formalism obliterates meaning and purpose, often to the point of transforming meaninglessness itself into a primary content. (1984, p. 33)

The San Francisco Mime Troupe has through good times and bad, straying sometimes perilously close to 'weak art', held on to its ideals, and in the process served as a model and an inspiration to the many similar groups and soloists that have followed.

Neither of the roads mentioned above, socialist art or formalism, has been able 'to reach the transformational center from which redemption comes', as Gablik describes it, yet it is just this transformational centre and this redemption that post-modernism reaches when it is successful.

Up to this point there has been some confusion between the words 'mime' and 'pantomime'. Now we are going to have trouble distinguishing among words such as 'actor', 'dancer', 'mime' and 'clown', since post-modernism is filled with hyphenated arts, two or three or four previously separated arts now combined in a synthesis appropriate to an age of instantaneous transmission of information, space travel, mass migrations and immigration, an age in which every action (and some might say every thought) is visibly connected to a larger whole, and where every time we turn on an electrical switch or drive down the road, the lives of individuals near and far are effected, as is the life of the planet.

For some, such as Douglas Paterson writing in *We are Strong: A Guide to Popular Theatre across the Americas*, the time has come to

announce a new age of theatre. It is time to defy Broadway and the universities. It is time to attack consumerism, chauvinism, and egoism, to expose irrelevance and faddish theatre gimmicks. It is time to leave the lights and the high tech and the bloated budgets for sets. It is time to abandon the cultural palaces – the Guthries, the ACTs [American Conservatory Theatre], the Juilliards, the cozy university/professional comforts, to abandon the provinciality of New York's avant-garde.

(1983, p. 2)

This perhaps strident rhetoric has been matched by action

in many alternative theatres, which have tried, and often succeeded, in developing progressive social and political consciousness both in co-operative ways of working and in the message of the work produced; in playing for a specific audience or in response to a specific political struggle; and in the members' desire to be part of the same community as their audience, rather than separate from them and exploiting them. The goal of alternative theatre has been to play for and with oppressed peoples, oppressed by race, sex, sexual preference, age, handicap, class or language.

The individual performers and collectives that identify themselves as alternative-theatre workers often use text taken from newspaper stories, interviews, government documents or other non-artistic sources. This text is broken open to reveal deeper meanings through mime, dance, magic, juggling, mask performance and puppets, bringing out themes which are ecological, feminist, radical political or economic. These themes often are specific to one city or region, are conducive to positive transformation and healing, and are satires of consumerism, or exposés of drug abuse, or teaching-pieces which point out the dangers inherent in other forms of anti-social, anti-planetary behaviour. In these performances mime, mask, myth, legend, marionette, vaudeville and circus blend in varying degrees from group to group and from production to production within groups. The message determines the medium.

These post-modernists condemn most modern theatre, protesting that it is the creation of, and primarily a depiction of, white men; post-modern theatre is about everyone and everything else.

There seem to be unmistakable political implications in the belief that one person writes, another acts, yet another directs, and someone else makes the costumes and the sets. Copeau did what he could to overcome the rigid professionalism that creates class distinctions and exploitation in Western theatre, making it a microcosm of the capitalist–industrialised world in which it exists. Yet this kind of rigid specialisation existed almost without being questioned for more than fifty years after Copeau first required his students to study all aspects of theatre, and still is the prevailing paradigm despite the alternative-theatre movement. As Arlene Goldbard asks in *We are Strong*, 'Should the industrial model of development be swallowed whole or is the cultural price it exacts too great?' (Paterson, 1983, p. 11). This is the kind of question alternative-theatre groups are asking themselves and their audiences. Most believe that cultural work has the ability to transform and heal individuals and the world.

7
New Vaudevillians, New Mimes

The famous pierrot Deburau ... had also been invited [to a party given by George Sand and Musset]. He arrived disguised as a visiting British politician, wearing a stiff collar and a long black coat, unrecognisable without his pierrot's costume and his chalk-white make-up. Throughout the dinner he maintained a truly English stiffness. ... Finally the phrase 'European equilibrium' was mentioned. The laconic Englishman showed a sudden interest. 'Do you wish to know how I view the European equilibrium in the present grave political situation between the continent and England?' he asked. 'If so, I will try to make myself clear.' And, picking up his plate, he spun it up into the air, catching it neatly on the tip of his knife where it continued to rotate at top speed. 'Such', he continued, 'is the present state of the

European equilibrium. There can be no salvation without it.' The astonished guests burst out laughing, the deception was revealed. . . .

This anecdote, told in Linda Kelly's *The Young Romantics* (1976, p. 86) demonstrates clearly the difference between the nineteenth-century white-faced pantomime artist's aesthetic and that of the late-twentieth-century new vaudevillian and new mime. Deburau could only unmask, speak and deal with the important issues of the day in private performance, playing a practical joke for his friends. For that one hour in the second half of the nineteenth century, he adumbrated what would happen in the second half of the twentieth.

The term 'new vaudeville' has begun to be used recently to describe that group of performers who descend, either directly or in spirit, from the San Francisco Mime Troupe. The Flying Karamazovs say new vaudeville was born on 7 June 1968, out of the political and artistic street life of the time. The Pickle Family Circus, San Francisco's one-ring alternative circus, was formed in 1974 by clown–juggler Larry Pisoni and designer–juggler Penny Snider, both formerly of the San Francisco Mime Troupe. Another one-ring, perhaps not-so-alternative circus grew out of the San Francisco Mime Troupe when member Paul Binder formed the Big Apple Circus, now a permanent resident of the Lincoln Center in New York.

The Pickle Family Circus, in its turn, has produced some alumni important in new vaudeville; among its former clowns are Bill Irwin and Geoff Hoyle, while juggler–mime–dancer Michael Moshen used to be a clown with the Big Apple, after having performed with the incomparable mime–dancer Lotte Goslar. Puppeteer–mime–storyteller Paul Zaloom was a member of the Bread and Puppet Theatre. If this narration seems circular, the relationships it describes certainly are.

Other prominent members of the New Vaudeville community are clown–mime Bob Berky, musician–composer–clown Keith Terry, Avner the Eccentric, Fred Garbo, and the Flying Karamazov Brothers. (See Jenkins, 1985.)

These individuals and a score of others work individually and together on projects which form and re-form in New York, in Los Angeles, in San Francisco and in Europe. Taking the discoveries of New Vaudeville back into mainstream theatre, Avner the Eccentric and the Karamazovs performed Shakespeare's *Comedy of Errors* in summer 1987.

Of the new vaudevillians, the one most in the public eye these days is Bill Irwin, who began in the acting-programme of the University of California at Los Angeles; undertook experimental theatre work with Herbert Blau at California Institute of the Arts and later at Oberlin, Ohio; attended the Ringling Brothers Clown College; worked as a clown with the Pickle Family; then joined the Oberlin Dance Collective before creating and performing in his own productions, among them *The Regard of Flight*. In 1984 Irwin won a MacArthur Fellowship, the first performer to be so honoured, which frees him from financial concern for a five-year period. Influenced by TV situation comedies (Phil Silvers, Burns and Allen, *The Honeymooners*), the movies of Keaton, Chaplin, W. C. Fields, the Marx Brothers and Abbott and Costello, and the legendary Swiss clown Grock, Irwin has devised his own brand of physical comedy which uses his abilities as a skilful mover (he calls himself an eccentric dancer), clown, juggler and actor–mime. Irwin, too, has taken his phenomenal skills back into mainstream theatre, appearing in productions of *The Seagull* (Chekhov) and *A Man's a*

Man (Brecht) at the La Jolla Playhouse in 1986. In the latter, he appeared with Geoff Hoyle, with whom he has also performed in plays by Dario Fo.

Irwin has on several occasions called new vaudeville 'American Kabuki'. In the Grand Kabuki's summer 1985 performances in the United States one could easily see why. The Kabuki, like new vaudeville, is a healthy theatre form. Neither pretends that everything can be expressed in text, or mime, or dance, or whatever, but both recognise that there are some moments when one is moved to song, dance or mime as the best way to express a texture, a feeling or a nuance of thought; both are theatres of synthesis, lively and colourful hyphenated theatres of dance–mime–juggling–acrobatics – and so on. Kabuki does not ask the audience to suspend its disbelief, although that inevitably happens at some moments during a performance. Kabuki actors sometimes call each other by their real names, refer to going offstage, 'behind that curtain there', and in other ways make us only too aware of the theatricality of what we are seeing. In *A Name-taking Ceremony*, they even humbly ask the audience to be their fans. New vaudeville, too, is oriented toward the audience in its frank theatricality, constantly breaking the fourth wall. A good portion of new vaudeville is about the act of performing, and *The Regard of Flight* is certainly about theatre-making in a post-modern world, or, as Kimi Okada described it, Irwin's work is about 'the nightmare of being a performer'.

Irwin, when asked for a statement about his work by *Mime Journal* in 1982, replied with two sentences. 'I work as a clown and as an actor. Since 1978, I have tried to put together contemporary theatre pieces which draw upon the older imagery of silent film, vaudeville and music hall clowning' (*New Mime in North America*, p. 93). In Irwin we see yet another artist going forward while looking back.

Another mime who began as a pure modernist and who discovered his own post-modernism is Leonard Pitt. In 1970 he left Paris, where he had for a long time been a student of Decroux, and moved to Berkeley, California, where he opened a mime school. For several years he practised and taught the mime technique he had learned in Paris, but with a vague feeling of dissatisfaction. Pitt remembers writing a note to himself during those early years in Berkeley and pinning it above his desk. It read, 'From the abstract to the concrete.' Decroux had spent years going from the concrete to the abstract during a period of analysis, but now, in a period of post-modern synthesis, Pitt said that he 'knew that one day the rarified world of corporeal mime would be behind me even though I had no idea of how or when this change would take place' (*New Mime in North America*, p. 132). After years of searching, experimenting with masks and percussion, Pitt witnessed a performance of Balinese music and dance. It changed the direction of his career; a few months later he went to Bali to study.

In Bali, Pitt found similarities and differences between what he had been working on in corporeal mime and the Balinese dance drama, but, more importantly, he found an art made from a synthesis of mime, dance, mask, acting, speech and music in a culture in which art and life were synthesised to the extent that there was no separate word for art. When he returned to Berkeley and his students, Pitt began to rework his understanding of corporeal mime, removing externals to find that the

nucleus consisted of physical skills and universal principles of movement that were based more on the intrinsic nature of the body, and its inherent necessities, than on a particular cultural bias of what the ideal body 'should' look like.   (*New Mime North America*, p. 137)

In the year following his return from Bali, Pitt formed a company and created a performance with movement expression at its base which integrated props, costume, masks, live percussion and dialogue. His own personal synthesis had begun. Through the study of mask-carving and acting, Pitt developed his solo performance *Dopo, Clown of Yesteryear*, in which he played an old French circus clown who spoke French with a wonderful Marseille accent. On the line from abstract to concrete, *Dopo* is about as far in the direction of the concrete as Pitt has gone; later, in his two collaborations with San Francisco performance artist George Coates, he turned back in a more abstract direction, but still in the context of a post-modern synthesis of theatrical elements. *2019 Blake*, a solo piece for Pitt directed by Coates, and *The Way of How*, a large group production with two opera singers, a mime (Pitt) and a musician–composer (Paul Dresher), combined, in Pitt's evaluation,

the values of the plastic arts with those of the performing arts to create strong stage events with a dominant visual and aural component. While the events are very precise in their visual and auditory content, we give them no predetermined meaning, nor do they follow a linear sequence. This allows the audience to fill in the blanks, so to speak, with their own meaning.

(*New Mime in North America*, p. 141)

This kind of performance resembles Trisha Brown's *Set and Reset* more than it does the work of the San Francisco

Mime Troupe, yet both are post-modernist in their synthesis of diverse and seemingly disparate elements. And, while the San Francisco Mime Troupe and similar theatres address political, environmental and ecological questions more directly and perhaps more forcefully, the underlying assumption in such a work as *The Way of How* is that we all share one planet and that people in life are interconnected in unusual, unexpected and important ways, just as sound and movement and colour are interconnected on the stage. 'We are not presenting a literal, linear picture of reality [in *The Way of How*]', Pitt explained. 'We're interested in playing with ambiguity, and we're interested in creating images that are tightly structured, that are very precise, but at the same time, very wide open' (Vreeland, 1984, p. 11). That's a description of the information age as well as a performance piece created in the information age.

The composer–musician for *The Way of How*, Paul Dresher, described his work in a 1985 programme note as follows:

The multiplicity of mediums in which Paul Dresher is presently working (chamber and orchestral compositions, experimental opera/musical theatre, and performances with his ensemble of musicians and live electronics) reflects the range of diverse styles and influences from which his music is formed. His work defies a single stylistic definition, drawing as it does from such seemingly disparate sources as non-western (particularly West African, Indonesian, and North Indian) traditions, European classical and renaissance musics, the experimental tradition of the 20th century, jazz, and rock and roll. From these Dresher is able to create a hybrid music that acknowledges the universal musical ideas and techniques at the core of the various traditions and styles but transcends the exotic surfaces of each.

That is as good a definition as one could hope to find of post-modernism, in its multi-ethnicity, its eclecticism, its non-linearity and its juxtaposition of disparate elements to form a resonant whole.

Milwaukee-born Daniel Stein was studying theatre in Pittsburgh at Carnegie-Mellon (with, among others, Jewel Walker, a student of Decroux's in the 1950s who has since specialised in actor-training) when he decided to take a year off to study in Wrocław with the Polish Mime Theatre. All packed and ready to go, he did not receive his visa in time, so he went to Paris instead. A gifted and successful white-faced pantomime performer on the street corners of Paris by night, Stein was an earnest student of Decroux by day. What he learned from Decroux in three years deepened his art. It took Stein two and a half years to assimilate Decroux's esoteric system into a personal statement, two and a half years from the end of his studies to the premiere of a clear, beautifully crafted theatre work entitled *Timepiece*. In 1978 at the Milwaukee Festival of American Mime, Daniel Stein gave the premiere of *Timepiece* outdoors on the fringe of the festival. That afternoon was a memorable one for the festival audience, mesmerised, despite the noise, the wind, the milling crowd, by a tall, slender, articulate young actor performing his heartfelt movement poem about the bittersweet passage of time, discovery, loss, and rediscovery of love. It is the kind of poem millions of late adolescents the world over write every year; the difference is that in Stein's composition the medium was beautifully crafted yet personalised corporeal-mime technique. His performance was startling because the content was deeply felt while the form was abstracted, though not beyond recognition.

Timepiece, on a literal level, depicted the inner workings of a clock, a Janus-masked combat, a bird, and a love duet performed by two chairs; Stein's metaphoric treatment took flight from those concrete points. Two chairs, a length of rope and a bamboo pole were manipulated in patterns that were satisfying both geometrically and dramatically. The galvanised audience demanded an encore, which was given indoors the next day on the main stage of the Milwaukee Performing Arts Center for a crowd that had grown in size and enthusiasm since the day before. Stein had walked away with the festival. Artists who had been struggling for years to figure out how to transcend the corporeal-mime technique were in two days given two stunning lessons. Audiences who didn't know what they were looking at were overwhelmed. The press responded enthusiastically, and the young man who had left Milwaukee a few years earlier looking for himself came back a young artist in full possession of his powers.

Stein toured *Timepiece* widely in the next few years to rave reviews. Sylvie Drake in the *Los Angeles Times* of 26 September 1978 called his performance 'one of those rare, revelatory experiences one waits for in the theatre', and she was reviewing what turned out to be only the fifth performance of the piece. Drake continued;

However abundant Stein's virtuosity may be (and it is), the presence of feeling in everything he does is what makes it so affecting. This marriage of craft and emotion, precision and pain, control and abandon is exceptional in this artist. The work is very pure, the variety of its physical compression seemingly infinite. It makes him a potentially direct heir to the Barrault–Marceau tradition.

Drake can be forgiven for not seeing that Stein had nothing in common with Barrault and Marceau except his talent; as they are the only two mimes of a certain quality almost anyone has seen anywhere, the confusion is understandable. Stein studied with Decroux long after Decroux had left that phase of his teaching which stressed illusions (objective mime) and from which Barrault and Marceau profited; Stein was a student of Decroux's riper years and stronger abstraction.

Dominique Paul Noth, writing in the *Milwaukee Journal*, was as impressed as the other critics who saw Stein perform in the years following the 1978 festival. But Noth was able to see something special about what the twenty-five-year-old Stein had done:

there are artists who seem a culmination of what has gone before and a direction for what will come after. Their creations have influence well beyond their lifetime or place of performance. With this work, Stein stands out as a prime hope for many explorers of modern theatre who have long seen the vague outline of a door but needed someone else to open it.

Janick Arbois-Chartier wrote in *Télérama* on 17 October 1979, 'Daniel Stein plays his body like a cello. . . . He does not tell little stories without words, he writes an overwhelming music of the body.'

Decroux once defined the mime performer as one possessing the mind of an actor, the heart of a poet and the body of a gymnast. Stein's superb acting finds expression in a well-articulated, supple body, trained in Decroux's technique and in classical ballet. But it is the poet that moves audiences to silence or to tears, and, at the end of *Timepiece*, to their feet.

Stein's second creation, *Scenes Apparent*, was premiered in New York at Dance Theatre Workshop in 1981. Jack Anderson, writing in the *New York Times* of 1 October, called Stein 'simultaneously a symbolist and an abstraction-ist' in explaining that Stein 'is fascinated by both the physical shape of objects and with what those objects may psychologically symbolize. And he is also interested in the patterns that objects make when they are set side by side.'

What Anderson may have identified here is the thing that makes Daniel Stein's work unique. He is an excellent animator of objects, and his object animation exists simultaneously on two levels. There is the level of pure design, and, in the first two of Stein's pieces mentioned here, as well as his later *Inclined to Agree*, the design elements of his body as well as of every prop and mask (designed by his wife, Paule Sandoval Stein) work beautifully together. One might find it difficult to take an unaesthetic photograph during one of Stein's perfor-mances, since every moment is carefully choreographed; abstract design has been well served. On the second level, there is the psychological meaning of Stein's gestures and movements, apart from their pure design quality. Stein's forte, then, is geometrically constructed yet referential movement.

Inclined to Agree is structurally Stein's most impressive creation so far, filling the stage with a veritable architecture of doors, windows, tables and chairs, all on the oblique. As a constant reprimand to this out-of-jointedness, there are 99 plumb-lines which occupy the same stage. The drama, of course, is what happens when these two obvious contradictions meet and try to resolve themselves in the person of the architect, Stein himself. A poem by Emily Dickinson, printed in the programme and recited by a woman's tape-recorded voice, helps in the resolution ('Tell all the truth, but tell it slant'). An image that remains in the mind long after the performance: truth (represented by the plumb-lines) has a shattering effect when its impact is felt – the rope supporting two of the plumb-bobs, stage left and stage right, is severed (by the architect's sudden revelation); they drop, and in so doing, break two panes of glass. Begun as a production of *Oedipus*, *Inclined to Agree* still has this vestige of the gouging-out of Oedipus's eyes. Oedipus searches for the truth, and, when he finally aligns himself with it, the truth blinds him. As the last lines of the Dickinson poem say 'The truth must dazzle gradually, / Or every man be blind.'

Stein is able to make a synthesis between the modernist pure abstractions and storytelling (via object animation) without falling into cuteness or the obvious. Stein has a school which, now that Decroux is no longer teaching, is among the few places in Paris where corporeal mime may be studied.

Two young performers and pedagogues, Steven Wasson and Corinne Soum, also have a school in Paris. Soum and Wasson, for a long time students and assistants of Decroux, presented their corporeal-mime play *The Crusade* at the International Festival of Contemporary Mime in Winnipeg in summer 1985 and in Montreal in summer 1986. They are well matched in their performance, both in technical virtuosity and in temperament. *The Crusade* is a wonderfully crafted collage of poignant images that seemed to be derived partly from the concentration camps of Nazi Germany, partly from the bureaucratisation of occupied France and the resonances those images have in modern

Europe. Soum explores the vocal and movement patterns of a young girl who meets the inflexibility of an adult world; Wasson, as an angel and other characters, is her nemesis–lover–saviour. *The Crusade* is an ambitious piece; it takes on some of the major issues of our time (the individual's relation to the state, for example) and illuminates them through the two actors' incisive movement and vocal explorations.

Jean Asselin and Denise Boulanger, already the directors of a mime troupe in Montreal, left Canada in 1972 and spent five years with Decroux in Paris. During their time with him, they acted as teaching assistants, translators and office people in the little school in Boulogne-Billancourt, just south of the Porte de Saint-Cloud. Of that time Jean Asselin wrote,

> In five years, things happen. And especially a technique, a thought are assimilated. I don't think that even this technique ever constituted the ultimate object of our thoughts and our voluntary gymnastic servitude.
>
> (*New Mime in North America*, p. 109)

Addressing the difficult problem of how to create using the corporeal-mime technique, Asselin commented,

> Yves Lebreton emphasizes the importance of unlearning in order to create. I understand and agree, but it should be clear that such a proposition can be addressed only to those who have learned.   (Ibid.)

Each of Decroux's students who stayed with him long enough to learn in depth (usually three to five years) faces the problem of 'unlearning in order to create'. This is how Asselin describes his solution:

With respect to the technique and teaching of corporeal mime, we try to disassociate them from Etienne Decroux. . . . I believe that Decroux's intent was always to create a vocabulary and a grammar appropriate to mime and capable of making it an autonomous art with respect to the other arts and his own person. But, if the technique of corporeal mime is perpetually associated with Etienne Decroux, the style with the man, he is done a disservice, and the most elementary gestural vocabulary is, at the same time, lost to us. Decroux's creations, his tastes and aesthetic needs are his affair. As for the technique, we make it our affair as teachers and practitioners. Decroux is not alone in the ivory tower in which some might like to enshrine him. Others as well believe in the poetic virtues of corporeal mime.

(Ibid., p. 110)

The works of Daniel Stein or Leonard Pitt are no more like the works of Jean Asselin than the poetry of three quite different poets is alike simply because they are writing in the same language. Asselin explains these differences:

Paradoxically, and in spite of our practicing this art, Decroux probably would not recognize a community of inspiration in the Omnibus repertory. This is because, at the same time that we are serving mime, we are using technique on behalf of our artistic intentions contained in each of our plays. (Ibid.)

Under Decroux's direction, Jean Asselin and Denise Boulanger developed three love duets (*Dieu les conduit*, *Ils regardent autre chose*, *La Déclaration*) in their five years with him. Their re-entry into the theatre was through

135

that ever-present agent of reintegration and synthesis, *commedia*. Premiered in 1977, *Zizi et la lettre* was Omnibus's first creation upon returning to Canada. A forty-five minute composition for nine characters and a spectacular circus tent, put up by the performers before the eyes of the audience in ninety seconds, this first post-Decroux theatre piece of course contained speech, 'an original esperanto vernacular composed of Italian, French, English, Voual (Quebec dialect), slang and any language or dialect depending on the nationality of the audience'. The degree of vocal mime and text in any work has varied from production to production; voice, like other 'alien arts', has been used when it was necessary, when nothing else would do. When Asselin writes, 'This play is completely irreverent about any historical truth as to what the real Commedia might have been' (*New Mime in North America*, p. 111), he sounds like Jacques Lecoq.

Since that beginning, Omnibus have explored any number of fruitful avenues of theatrical research, never turning back or settling on the formula that worked in the previous play.

> 'Multinational collective' expresses rather well what our creations have been since 1977; artists of seven different nationalities have participated in our creations since that time, creations which are inherently collective. It could not be otherwise because our dramatic system is rooted in the way of being, and thus the exploitation, of people at their most private level. Multinationality immunizes us against any form of cultural chauvinism. Omnibus is apolitical. (Ibid., p. 113)

While Bill Irwin is acting Chekhov and the Flying Karamzovs Shakespeare, Omnibus have taken on texts by prominent French Canadian and European authors.

Another outstanding Montreal-based theatre artist who had his beginnings in the Decroux school is Gilles Maheu, founder and artistic director of Carbonne 14, a troupe which began in 1975 under the name 'Les Enfants du Paradis'. The troupe's first widely performed creation, entitled *Le Voyage immobile* (the title reminds one of Decroux quoting Chaplin: 'Mime is immobility transported'), was a work of great power which unfolded as slowly, and was as delicately coloured, as the little paper flowers sealed between two halves of a small seashell that we used to buy as children, drop into a glass of water and watch blossom. It was as if Maheu dropped a nugget of pure memory onto the stage, and, in that special, attentive silence, some important part of his childhood came unstuck and flowered into art before us. The story was simple – a birth, a childhood, a passage into adulthood and a death. It was not what was done, but how it was done, that audiences everywhere found deeply moving. One critic wrote, "I can't recall being moved to tears before in the theatre. . . . We do not expect to be overcome by emotion as purely as if we had sat down with a friend, who quietly and eloquently revealed some shattering, personal truth"' (Lord, 1979).

Like their sister company Omnibus, Carbonne 14 love scenic as well as corporeal imagery, and *Le Voyage immobile* was sumptuously appointed. Each detail of the costuming, which perfectly evoked a North American ambience of the 1950s, was accurate and had a super-real sheen, like the hyper-realistic masks the actors wore. Watching the background of gold satin curtains, which moved as articulately as the actors themselves, the gently glowing (as if from within), shimmering costume materials, the glint on the baby-buggy chrome, and the high-gloss sheen on the shoes, one knew that each moment on the stage and each detail of the production, down to the soft, black velour-covered floor, was loved, cherished and respected by the actors. The production stays in the memory. One unforgettable moment: the young man, played by Gilles Maheu, *almost* makes a gesture. Years later, the incompleteness, the intention that never reached its goal, the unconnected suspension points still hang in the air. *Le Voyage immobile* was like a North American Nō play in its highly charged understatement.

Since *Le Voyage immobile*, Carbonne 14 have gone on to produce many successful theatre productions as well as street events with a shifting cast of actors and other collaborators as the work requires. They have, like Omnibus, performed throughout Canada, and widely in Europe, but infrequently in the United States. In summer 1987, they, like their post-modern colleagues, were working with text: Gilles Maheu's choice was Heiner Müller's *Hamlet-Machine*.

Montreal has, over the past ten years, become an important place for post-modern mime. There are a large number of mimes trained by Decroux and his students there, and the government subsidy (often 50 per cent or more of company budgets) has encouraged the kind of deep and wide experimentation that has been impossible in the United States or in Europe. The presence of companies such as Omnibus and Carbonne 14, the Omnibus school and independent teachers such as George Molnar and André Fortin, mime critics such as Aline Gélinas, and a growing, knowledgeable mime audience combine to make Montreal of world importance.

The Adaptors, a Brooklyn-based company formed by Tony Brown and Kari Margolis, performed their first work, *Autobahn*, in June 1984 at the International Festival of Mime and Clown in Elkins, West Virginia. Brown and Margolis, after study in Paris with Decroux, were members of the first Omnibus troupe in Montreal, where they had lessons first-hand in the assimilation of corporeal-mime technique into a theatrical event. In a letter to me, Brown and Margolis wrote, 'Technique is the link between the soul of the artist and the mind of the spectator. Our fascination with technique has grown into a fascination with the potential of the human instrument.' Like Jean Asselin and Denise Boulanger, Margolis and Brown are teachers as well as performers. In their teaching of Decroux technique as well as improvision, they ask an actor to move across the room:

With each step he/she is to concentrate on feeling heavier and heavier. On arriving at the center of the room, the actor is to emote muscularly what the journey has evoked. One actor is lost, void of emotion and direction; another is transformed and we are moved by the improvisation. This actor has entered the hyper-reality of 'the creative state'. The muscular sensation of the journey stimulated the actor emotionally and intellectually. In this 'creative state' the actor found the form and the meaning in the improvisation, exciting him/herself and us. (Letter)

Like Omnibus and Carbonne 14, the Adaptors (the name itself implies synthesis and integration) enjoy the theatricality of the 'alien arts' and use them liberally. 'We see a distinction between a theatre piece that employs movement and a mime piece that employs the tools of the theatre', Brown and Margolis said. This is certainly the spirit in which Decroux undertook his work – a house-cleaning for the theatre, and the re-establishment of the actor in the primary place.

Autobahn is a satirical collage of life in contemporary America; the title suggests something about life in the fast lane. One reviewer described it as

> a kind of post-modernist political cabaret, which drives its points home through strong formal elements that do an end-run around our conventional intellectual understanding. The opening number presents the pointless panorama of American endeavor moving toward the climactic moment when the wieners are finally barbecued. (Skene, 1985)

Another reviewer remarked that the 'eleven cabaretlike scenes . . . take a fast tour through the progress of technology since World War II, viciously mocking American consumerism by celebrating it with the insane cheerfulness of TV testimonial commercials' (Shewey, 1985). Like a modern *commedia* troupe, the Adaptors are using the abundant subject matter around them, commenting directly on the culture they are a part of, reflecting it, and in the process changing what they reflect.

Another graduate of Decroux's school, via the first Omnibus company, is Dulcinea Langfelder, an American whose solo *The Circle*, performed at the Festival of Contemporary Mime in Winnipeg in 1985, is a rigorous physical and intellectual exploration of that geometric shape. Langfelder embodies archetypes which call to mind everything from Shiva balanced on one foot inside a flaming hoop to faded black-and-white photographs of pioneer American modern dancer Doris Humphrey suspended in a circle of movement surrounded by a circle of wood.

Performing artist Jan Munroe worked with Decroux in

140

the early 1970s before moving first to San Francisco and later to Los Angeles, where he now lives. Munroe questions whether what he does can accurately be called mime.

> I only know where I started, that I am thankful for the multi-faced base that working with Decroux gave me (not just his movement, but the sense of poetry, philosophy, and humor that flowed through him) and that has enabled me to step out in these different directions. As Decroux once said in a lecture, 'I give what I can to my students and leave the rest to God.'
> (*New Mime in North America*, p. 102)

Munroe has created solo and small-group performance pieces that have included music, video, dance, and elements of text. Among Munroe's productions, the long-running *Alligator Tales and Other Appendages*, an evening of movement and autobiographical storytelling, is an evocation of the sights and smells of growing up near the swamps of north Florida. While some post-modern mimes are now performing plays written by others, Jan Munroe's *Alligator Tales* has been published in an anthology of new West Coast plays, and he has been awarded a Rockefeller Foundation Playwright Grant.

Not all recent Decroux-based work follows the same pattern. Bert Houle and Veera Wibaux of San Francisco have made their synthesis by doing an evening of solo and duet works which use illusionistic pantomime and *commedia* techniques in one part of the programme and the more abstract, subjective mime on the other. In recent years they have sometimes abandoned this format to create full performance-length dramatic compositions with groups of their students.

Marguerite Mathews is developing a resident corporeal-mime repertory theatre in Portsmouth, New Hampshire. Whereas most of the performers mentioned in this chapter develop one new work every year or two which they perform nationally and internationally, Marguerite Mathews produces several new works a year in one location for a primarily local and regional audience. Her theatre is called Pontine, and is usually composed of three or four corporeal mimes aside from herself, exploring a wide range of movement theatre and experimenting with text, music and masks.

Another primarily community-based group is the Friends Mime Theatre of Milwaukee, founded in 1973 by Barbara Leigh and Michael Moynihan. FMT specialises in performances in parking-lots, churches, prisons, centres for senior citizens, and so on, as well as in theatres. The content of their work focuses on 'social issues, change itself, and the mythical consciousness of our everyday lives' but derives much from *commedia*, Kabuki and mime for its form. Like other alternative-theatre groups, FMT has as its primary goal a theatre that could 'transform its creators as well as the audience experiencing it' (letter from Barbara Leigh).

One of the most overtly political groups I consider in this chapter is the United Mime Workers, of Champaign, Illinois. For more than ten years they managed their company by themselves, did everything from booking to costumes, as is customary with many alternative-theatre groups. Bob Feldman, Deborah Langerman, Jeff Glassman and Candace Walworth performed works which challenged audiences to examine the economic and political realities of their daily lives. Their training came from a synthesis of mime, Kabuki and musical-composition techniques. These artists now work as individuals, the

United Mime Workers having dissolved in 1986.

There are literally hundreds of other artists in the United States and Canada whose work would serve to illustrate the basic ideas we have been examining about the nature of new mime and new vaudeville. From among hundreds of European groups which do the same, I have chosen the following representatives.

Grifteater is one of the many mime and movement-theatre groups active in Holland, which, like Canada, is a centre for theatrical innovation because of its government subsidy to artists. Freed from the necessity to stage performances with a wide popular appeal, these groups are forging new directions in visual theatre. Artistic director Frits Vogels proposes Grifteater's plotless theatre as

> a counterweight, not to replace story theatre, but to show that through the eye and ear the senses can be touched directly. Noticing space can cause an essential emotion. During a performance that tells a story through words and characters, these points are easily over-looked. (*New Mime in Europe*, p. 162)

Since its founding in 1975, almost all of Grifteater's productions have taken their name from the visual arts, inspired by light, colour, space and movement. Vogels explains that 'Psychological development or a prepared dramaturgy is not the center of the production, but the images themselves, created by the actors in combination with space and objects, are the primary focus' (ibid., p. 167).

Poland and Czechoslovakia have old and vital mime traditions, which have grown because of government subsidy and despite government control. The Polish Mime-

Ballet Theatre, directed by Henryk Tomaszewski, produces elaborately costumed and ornately decorated neo-baroque productions performed by heavily muscled, well-oiled actors and actresses often clad in the smallest bits of gold lame. Tomaszewski's expressive movement vocabulary, a hybrid of mime and ballet, is an important development in a country in which modern dance is almost unknown. It is difficult to imagine that the stark expressionistic anguish of Jerzy Grotowski and the jewelled fantasy of Tomaszewski coexisted for many years in the industrial city of Wrocłow.

Czechoslovaika's Ladislav Fialka has for decades produced traditional silent mimodramas in a charming little theatre in Prague and less frequently abroad, while the younger mime artist Boleslav Polivka performs his post-modern clown shows many months of the year in Western Europe and North America. Polivka is an Eastern European new vaudevillian, as are Ctibor Turba and Boris Hybner, who perform in Czechoslovakia and less often abroad.

New vaudeville seems to be an American invention, although there are actors from other countries aside from Polivka who perform in many different styles, often within the same performance, incorporating text, costumes, props and other theatrical elements. West German F. J. Bogner and the Argentinian Benito Gutmacher are what might be called post-modern anti-mimes who owe more to Artaud than they do to Marceau.

Mime festivals have become important in the last decade in the promulgation of the art. Several impresarios have played signal roles in broader public acceptance of new mime and new vaudeville. Some of these individuals are Peter Bu in France, Joseph Seelig in England, Robert Dion in Montreal, Giuseppe Condello in Winnipeg,

Wayne Specht in Vancouver, Sigfrido Aquilar in Guana-juato, Mexico, David White in New York City and Michael Pedretti in Philadelphia.

Jan Ruts's Pyramide op de Punt is based in Antwerp, Belgium. *Het Zuilenveld* (*The Colony*) has been performed to critical acclaim at festivals throughout Europe and in Canada. For Ruts it is

> important to realize that mime has become corporeal mime. This corporeality of mime makes it an art *par exellence* of the pre- and post-verbal world. That is to say, worlds which escape us because they are in-comprehensible and incommunicable by established language. And that is why, in fact, theatre exists: to express these states of being.
>
> (*New Mime in Europe*, p. 168)

Ruts studied with Decroux, whose 'technique as much as his philosophy gave mimes the possibility to direct their work toward the very heart of theatre' (ibid.). Ruts believes that Decroux's work has actualised in our time the theory that speculates that theatre rediscovers its origins in mime, develops itself in speech toward another level, which is corporeal, and the starting place for further development. This theory resembles that of analysis and synthesis with which we began this study.

Théâtre du Movement, Claire Heggen and Yves Marc, also educated by Etienne Decroux, identify their work as 'contemporary rather than recreating romantic themes from classical pantomime' (*New Mime in Europe*, 174). Both formerly teachers of physical education, Heggen was trained as a modern dancer as well as a mime, and Marc is an athlete and dancer as well as a mime. Théâtre du Movement has in recent years grown to a company of six performers. Their territory is that of the other performers mentioned in this chapter, the festivals of Europe and North America, the small fringe theatres in major cities and medium sized theatres in smaller cities.

They have expressed their goal this way:

> We would like to transform ourselves. Mime and many-shapedness seem the goal to attain, until we discover how, through our work, to change our own and our audience's perception of things.   (177)

A recurrent theme throughout post-modern performance is the work of transformation, physical and metaphysical, domestic and planetary. The post-modern mime transforms and shapes his body not as a sign or symbol for some word he has chosen not to speak, or as a complement to a word he had chosen to speak, but as a metaphor for some other transformation, some other shaping, that can not be seen, but which can be hinted at through the visible.

The voyage from Copeau's theatre on the rue du Vieux Colombier in the early part of the twentieth century to its successors all over the world at the end of the same century has been the subject of these chapters. It has been said that each of us is continually writing his own history, constantly revising the past in an attempt to make it useful and coherent. If that is true, these chapters have been as much a portrait of my own development, from the synthesised play-making of childhood, through the studied modernist classicism of late adolesence and early adulthood, back again to a full synthesis of voice, movement, colour and story. These chapters have been composed from the material I have had at hand; anyone else would have seen this history with different eyes, and would have written a different book.

Bibliography

Anders, France, *Jacques Copeau et le Cartel des quatre* (Paris: A. G. Nizet, 1959).

Arbois-Chartier, Janick, review of Daniel Stein's *Timepiece* in *Télérama*, 17 Oct. 1979.

Artaud, Antonin, *Lettres d'Antonin Artaud à Jean-Louis Barrault* (Paris: Bordas, 1952).

——, *The Theatre and its Double*, tr. Mary Caroline Richards (New York: Grove Press, 1958).

Barba, Eugenio, 'Theatre Anthropology', *Drama Review*, 26, no. 2 (1982) pp. 5–32.

Barrault, Jean-Louis, 'Child of Silence', tr. Eric Bentley, *Theatre Arts*, Oct. 1949, pp. 28–31.

——, *Nouvelles Réflexions sur le théâtre* (Paris: Flammarion, 1959).

——, *Reflections on the Theatre*, tr. Barbara Wall (London: Rockliff, 1951).

——, *Saisir le présent* (Paris: Robert Laffont, 1984).

——, *Souvenirs pour demain* (Paris: Editions du Seuil, 1972).

——, *Une Troupe et ses auteurs* (Paris: Jacques Vautrain, 1950).

——, 'Le Corps magnétique', *Cahiers Renaud Barrault*, 99 (1979) pp. 71–135.

Bellugue, Paul, *A propos d'art de forme et de mouvement* (Paris: Librairie Maloine, n.d.).

Bentley, Eric, theatre review in *New Republic*, 10 Oct. 1955, p. 21.

Bibliography

——, 'The Pretensions of Pantomime', *Theatre Arts*, Feb. 1951, pp. 26–30.

Brown, Frederick, *Theatre and Revolution* (New York: The Viking Press, 1980).

Buhrer, Michel, *Mummenschanz* (Lausanne: Editions Pierre-Marcel Favre, 1984).

Carlson, Marvin, 'The Golden Age of the Boulevard', *Drama Review*, 18, no. 1 (1974) pp. 25–33.

Carné, Marcel, *Les Enfants du Paradis* (*Children of Paradise*), tr. Dinah Brooke (London: Lorrimer, 1968).

Clark, Kenneth, *The Nude* (Princeton, N.J.: Princeton University Press, 1956).

Cocuzza, Ginnine, review of Mummenschanz in *Mime News*, May–June 1979.

Clurman, Harold, 'Theatre', *Nation*, 29 Oct. 1955, p. 370.

Champfleury, Jules Fleury, *Souvenirs et portraits de jeunesse* (Paris: E. Dentu, 1872).

Copeau, Jacques, *Souvenirs du Vieux-Colombier* (Paris: Les Nouvelles Editions Latines, 1931).

——, 'Notes on the Actor', tr. Harold J. Salemson, in *Actors on Acting*, ed. Toby Cole and Helen Kirch Chinoy (New York: Crown Publishers, 1970) pp. 216–25.

——, *Appels* (Paris: Gallimard, 1974).

——, *Les Registres du Vieux Colombier I* (Paris: Gallimard, 1979).

——, *Les Registres du Vieux Colombier II* (Paris: Gallimard, 1984).

Craig, Gordon, 'Enfin un créateur au théâtre', *Empreintes*, 4 (Jan. 1980) pp. 55–6.

Dasté, Jean, *Voyage d'un comédien* (Paris: Stock, 1977).

Decroux, Etienne, *Words on Mime*, tr. Mark Piper (Claremont, Calif.: Mime Journal, 1985).

Disher, M. Willson, *Clowns and Pantomimes* (London: Constable, 1925).

Dobbels, Daniel, 'Mime et Mimes' (interview with Jean-Louis Barrault), *Empreintes*, 4 (Jan. 1980) pp. 48–54.

Dorcy, Jean, *A la rencontre de la mime* (Neuilly-sur-Seine: Les Cahiers de Danse et Culture, 1958).

——, *The Mime*, tr. Robert Speller Jr and Marcel Marceau (London: White Lion, 1961).

——, *J'aime la mime* (Lausanne: Editions Rencontre, 1962).

Drake, Sylvie, review of Daniel Stein's *Timepiece*, *Los Angeles Times*, 26 Sept. 1978.

Epstein, Alvin, 'The Mime Theatre of Etienne Decroux', *Chrysalis*, XI, 1/2 (1958).

Fago, John, 'Bread and Puppet', *Christian Science Monitor*, 16 Aug. 1985.

Fleishman, Philip, 'The Gift of Creation, an interview with Marcel Marceau', *Atlas World Press Review*, Aug. 1978, pp. 26–7.

Feinsod, Arthur, 'Marceau's Bip and the Creation of a Stage Persona', unpublished.

Foster, Hal (ed.), *The Anti-Aesthetic* (Port Townsend, Wash.: Bay Press, 1983).

Fowlie, Wallace, *Dionysus in Paris* (New York: Meridian Books, 1960).

Frank, André, *Jean-Louis Barrault* (Paris: Editions Seghers, 1971).

Gablik, Suzi, *Has Modernism Failed?* (New York: Thames and Hudson, 1984).

Gascar, Pierre, *Le Boulevard du crime* (Paris: Atelier Hachette/Massin, 1980).

Gelabert, Raoul, 'Etienne Decroux has Much to Teach Us', *Dance Magazine*, Sept. 1959.

Gide, André, *The Journals of André Gide*, vol. III: 1928–39, tr. Justin O'Brian (New York: Alfred A. Knopf, 1949).

Gill, Brendan, 'The Theatre: Friends', *New Yorker*, 28 Mar. 1983, p. 110.

Gillespie, John K., 'Interior Action: The Impact of Noh on Jean-Louis Barrault', *Comparative Drama*, Winter 1982/83, pp. 325–44.

Gilman, Richard, 'Theatre: Marcel Marceau on Broadway', *The Nation*, 2 April 1983.

——, 'The Stage: Marceau: The Limits of Illusion', *Commonweal*, 25 Jan. 1963.

Goldberg, Roselee, *Performance: Live Art 1909 to the Present* (London: Thames and Hudson, 1979).

Grotowski, Jerzy, *Towards a Poor Theatre* (New York: Simon and Schuster, 1968).

Hausbrandt, Andrzej, *Tomaszewski's Mime Theatre* (Warsaw: Interpress, 1975).

Hastings, Lily and Baird, 'The New Mime of Etienne Decroux', *Dance Magazine*, Sept. 1951.

Hatch, Robert, review of Marcel Marceau, *Nation*, 8 Feb. 1958, p. 126.

Hayes, Richard, 'The Stage: The Overreacher', *The Commonweal*, 7 Oct. 1960, pp. 45–6.

——, 'The Stage: The Renaud-Barrault Company', *The Commonweal*, 5 Dec. 1952, 223.

——, 'The Stage: The French Lesson', *Commonweal*, 21 Oct. 1953, pp. 62–3.

Herondas, *The Mimes of Herondas*, tr. Guy Davenport (San Francisco: Grey Fox Press, 1981).

Jenkins, Ron, 'Acrobats of the Soul', *American Theatre*, Mar. 1985, pp. 4–11.

Bibliography

Kaufmann, Stanley, 'Old-New and New-Old', *New Republic*, 16 Dec. 1978, p. 20.

Kelly, Linda, *The Young Romantics* (London: Bodley Head, 1976).

Kroll, Jack, 'Pratfalls and Politics', *Newsweek*, 22 Jan. 1973, p. 65.

Kuhn, Thomas, S., *The Structure of Scientific Revolutions* (Chicago: University of Chicago Press, 1970).

Leabhart, Thomas (ed.), *Etienne Decroux 80th Birthday Issue* of *Mime Journal* (1978).

Lecoq, Jacques, 'Le corps et son espace', *Notes méthodologiques en architecture et urbanisme*, no. 3/4 (Jan. 1974) pp. 273–81.

Leigh, Barbara Kusler, *Jacques Copeau's School for Actors* (Allendale, Mich.: *Mime Journal*, 1979).

Lerminier, Georges, *J. Copeau* (Paris: Les Presses Littéraires de France, 1953).

Levy, Alan, 'A Week avec Lecoq', *Mime, Mask and Marionette*, 1 (1978) pp. 45–62.

Lewis, Maggie, interview with Merce Cunningham in *The Christian Science Monitor*, 9 May 1979, 20.

Lorant, Terry and Carroll, Jon, *The Pickle Family Circus* (San Francisco: Chronicle Books, 1986).

Lord, Sarah Fenno, 'Illusion and Reality', *Columbia Flyer* (Baltimore), 15 Nov. 1979.

Lorelle, Yves, *L'Expression corporelle* (Paris: La Renaissance du Livre, 1974).

Marceau, Marcel, 'The Language of the Heart', *Theatre Arts* (Mar. 1958) pp. 58–70.

——, 'Bip sur les chemins de l'actualité', *Lettres françaises*, 8 Oct. 1969.

——, 'Who am I?', *Dance Magazine*, Nov. 1965, pp. 49–51.

Martin, Ben, *Marcel Marceau Master of Mime* (New York: Paddington Press, 1978).

McLean, Francis, unpublished interview with Jacques Lecoq, tr. Francis McLean and Graham Valentin, 26 April 1980.

Méricot, Jacques, *Recherches historiques et critiques sur les mimes et sur les pantomimes* (Paris, 1751).

Mignon, Paul-Louis, *Jean Dasté* (Paris: Les Presses Littéraires de France, 1953).

New Mime in Europe, in *Mime Journal*, 1983.

New Mime in North America, in *Mime Journal*, 1980–2.

Nicoll, Allardyce, *Masks, Mimes and Miracles* (New York: Cooper Square, 1963).

Noth, Dominique Paul, review of Daniel Stein's *Timepiece* in *Milwaukee Journal*, 3 Sept. 1978.

Okada, Kimi, quoted in 'Profiles: Clown' by Mel Gussow, *New Yorker*, 11 Nov. 1985, p. 68.

Oliver, Edith, 'Off Broadway: Mummers', *New Yorker*, 11 April 1977.

Olsen, Birgit, unpublished interview with M. H. Dasté, 20 Feb. 1976.

Paterson, Douglas, *We Are Strong: A Guide to Popular Theatre across America* (Mankato, Minn.: Institute for Cultural Policy Studies, 1983).

Rolfe, Bari (ed.), *Mimes on Miming* (Los Angeles: Panjandrum Books, n.d.).

——, 'Magic Century of French Mime', *Mime, Mask & Marionette*, 1 (1978), pp. 135–58.

——, 'Masks, Mime and Mummenschanz', *Mime Journal*, 2 (1975) pp. 24–35.

——, 'The Mime of Jacques Lecoq', *Drama Review*, 16, no. 1 (1972) pp. 34–8.

Root-Berstein, Michele, *Boulevard Theatre and Revolution in Eighteenth Century Paris* (Ann Arbor: University of Michigan Research Press, 1984).

Rudlin, John, *Jacques Copeau* (Cambridge: Cambridge University Press, 1986).

Saint-Denis, Michel, *Theatre: The Rediscovery of Style* (New York: Theatre Arts Books, 1969).

Shawn, Ted, *Every Little Movement* (Pittsfield, Mass.: Eagle Printing, 1954).

Shewey, Don, 'The Marriage of Junk and Myth', *The Village Voice*, 18 June 1985.

Siegel, Marcia, *Watching the Dance Go By* (Boston, Mass.: Houghton Mifflin, 1977).

Skene, Reg, 'Theatrical Mime Troupe Electrifies', *Winnipeg Free Press*, 7 June 1985.

Souriau, Paul, *The Aesthetics of Movement*, tr. and ed. by Manon Souriau with foreword by Francis Sparshott (Amherst: University of Massachusetts Press, 1983).

Stebbins, Genevieve, *Delsarte System of Expression* (New York: Dance Horizons, 1977).

Stoop, Norma McLain, 'The Interior Music of Marcel Marceau', *Dance Magazine*, July 1975.

Toscan, Richard and Ripley, Kathryn, 'The San Francisco Mime Troupe: Commedia to Collective Creation', *Theatre Quarterly*, 5, no. 18 (1975) p. 22.

Updike, John, 'Books: Modernists, Postmodernists, What Will They Think of Next?', *New Yorker*, 10 Sept. 1984, pp. 136–42.

Vreeland, Nancy, 'Next Wave Mime', *Dance Magazine*, 19 Jan. 1984.

Waley, Arthur, *The Nō Plays of Japan* (New York: Alfred A. Knopf, 1922).

Bibliography

Weiss, William, 'An Interview with Jean-Louis Barrault', *Mime, Mask & Marionette* II, 1 (1979) pp. 1–11.

Winter, Marian Hannah, 'The Repertoire of Marcel Marceau and Company', *Dance Magazine*, May 1959, pp. 52–5, 80.

Wolff, Theodore F., 'Art in Our Century, Part I', *Christian Science Monitor*, 24 Oct. 1985, pp. 18–19.

Wylie, Lawrence, 'A l'école Lecoq j'ai découvrert mon propre clown', *Psychologie*, Aug. 1973, pp. 17–27.

Index